Tattooing and the Gender Turn

Emerald Studies in Popular Culture and Gender

Series Editor: Samantha Holland, Leeds Beckett University, UK

As we re-imagine and re-boot at an ever faster pace, this series explores the different strands of contemporary culture and gender. Looking across cinema, television, graphic novels, fashion studies and reality TV, the series asks: what has changed for gender? And, perhaps more seriously, what has not? Have representations of genders changed? How much does the concept of 'gender' in popular culture define and limit us?

We not only consume cultural texts but also share them more than ever before; meanings and messages reach more people and perpetuate more understandings (and misunderstandings) than at any time in history. This new series interrogates whether feminism has challenged or changed misogynist attitudes in popular culture.

Emerald Studies in Popular Culture and Gender provides a focus for writers and researchers interested in sociological and cultural research that expands our understanding of the ontological status of gender, popular culture and related discourses, objects and practices.

Available Titles in This Series

Gender and Action Films 2000 and Beyond: Transformations – Edited by Steven Gerrard and Renée Middlemost

Gender and Action Films: Road Warriors, Bombshells and Atomic Blondes – Edited by Steven Gerrard and Renée Middlemost

Gender and Action Films 1980–2000: Beauty in Motion – Edited by Steven Gerrard and Renée Middlemost

Forthcoming Titles in This Series

Gender, True Crime and Criminology: Offenders, Victims, and Ethics – Authored by Louise Wattis

Gender and the Male Character in 21st Century Fairy Tale Narratives – Edited by Natalie Le Clue

Tattooing and the Gender Turn: Labour, Resistance and Activism in a Male-Dominated Industry

BY

EMMA BECKETT

University of Warwick, UK

United Kingdom – North America – Japan – India – Malaysia – China

Emerald Publishing Limited
Emerald Publishing, Floor 5, Northspring, 21-23 Wellington Street, Leeds LS1 4DL

First edition 2023

Reprints and permissions service
Contact: permissions@emeraldinsight.com

British Library Cataloguing in Publication Data
A catalogue record for this book is available from the British Library

ISBN: 978-1-80262-302-4 (Print)
ISBN: 978-1-80262-301-7 (Online)
ISBN: 978-1-80262-303-1 (Epub)

Printed and bound by CPI Group (UK) Ltd, Croydon, CR0 4YY

INVESTOR IN PEOPLE

For Sid and Woodrow –
may you grow into fierce feminist allies.

Table of Contents

About the Author

Emma Beckett is a Lecturer in Health and Social Care at New College, Swindon (UK), and an honorary research fellow in the Centre for the Study of Women and Gender at the University of Warwick (UK). Her research interests include Sub-cultures; Gendered and Emotional Labour and Gendered Capital – specifically within the service industries and traditionally 'male' dominated spaces; and the Sociology of Health. Emma is also interested in exploring ways in which feminist activism and feminist pedagogy can be successfully employed in the classroom.

Acknowledgements

My first thanks go to the wonderful tattoo artists who were so generous with their time and conversation, without whom this book would not have been possible. I enjoyed the fieldwork so much and was incredibly lucky to speak to some truly amazing people.

Dr Nikki Rivers – it is hard to put into words how thankful I am. A confidant, counsellor, proof-reader, hilarity provider – this book would not have been possible without her, and she will never truly know how appreciative I am, for so many things.

Thank you to Dr Samantha Holland for inspiring me with 'Alternative Femininities' all those years ago, and since then, believing in this book, and championing my research – the support and positivity means so much.

I would like to thank Dr Maria do Mar Pereira, whose encouragement, inspiration and motivation gave me the confidence to develop my ideas into something I am proud of – I am extremely grateful for all that Maria has brought to this project over very many years!

Behind every woman there is a gang of warrior women, raising her up and rooting for her, and for this I'd like to thank Abby, Ioana, Gosia, Sarah, Tessa, Tammy, my sister Lucy and step-mum Amanda for years of endless laughter, friendship and encouragement.

Thank you to my Dad, Alan, for normalising tattoos for me and never judging me in whatever choices I've made. And to The Greens (all of you!) for always being there when I have needed you.

Thank you also, to The Sociological Support Goop (spelling intended) – Dr Liz Ablett, Dr Carli Ria Rowell, Dr Iro Konstantinou and Dr Sara Bamdad – for your reassurance, motivation and continuous belief that we are capable and good enough. Thank you.

Finally – I would like to thank my Mum, Chris, for her endless and unconditional belief and support – she is a constant inspiration to me and someone to whom I am forever grateful.

And Thom – far too many things to be thankful for… thank you.

Chapter 1

From Freak Shows to Feminism

Introduction

I grew up surrounded by tattoos; my dad, uncles and grandads were all tattooed. As a little girl growing up in a working-class family in 1980s Britain, being surrounded by tattooed family was normal, and not something I ever remember questioning and yet I always attribute my love of tattoos and body modification to my affiliation with alternative subcultures and music. The tattoos I saw on my family felt very different to the world of tattooing I would become so familiar with years later, but the normalising of body modification amongst my family must have had an impact upon the way I thought about tattoos from a very early age – even if I didn't know it at the time.

When, aged 18, I walked into a tattoo studio ready to get tattooed for the first time, I felt like I was entering a different world. A world that I had been peering into from afar until that moment – reading magazines, studying the tattoos of my musician idols, planning and drawing designs on myself with a pen. When I stood outside the studio with the tattooist, post-tattoo, I felt like I'd finally made it into 'the club'. I couldn't wait to show my tattoo off, further declaring my 'difference' to the mainstream along with my developing love of subcultures. As my tattoo collection grew, and my affiliation with the world of tattooing developed, the feeling of belonging to *something bigger than myself* was amplified. I was also developing a connection with alternative music, specifically grunge, punk and subsequently, riot grrrl culture. I was experiencing first-hand, the emotions of being on the peripheries of the mainstream and at the same time, a sense of belonging to something offering an alternative.

When I returned to the same studio to get my second tattoo, not long after my first, I was told that the artist, whom I met previously, had been asked to leave – he had exposed himself to a customer. I was 19 years old, being told about a man much older than myself, exposing himself to someone who had presumably trusted him, and weirdly, I don't remember being shocked by this. Was this just *something that happened* in tattoo studios?

From my experience of being tattooed, and spending time in studios, I became all-too aware that tattooed women experience the community, and wider society, very differently to tattooed men. I was also aware, therefore, that women tattoo artists, queer artists and/or artists of colour were likely to experience the industry

Tattooing and the Gender Turn, 1–16
Copyright © 2023 Emma Beckett
Published under exclusive licence by Emerald Publishing Limited
doi:10.1108/978-1-80262-301-720231001

in a very different way to their straight, white, male colleagues. I knew that the industry had been a very male-dominated field for a long time. I have visited enough studios – heavily male-dominated studios – to have been privy to the 'banter' clients endure whilst getting tattooed and have experienced this whilst getting tattooed myself. Sexist jokes, sexualised comments and innuendos are not uncommon in male-dominated spaces and tattoo studios are certainly no exception. The term *banter* does not always sit comfortably with me as it is often used to excuse offensive comments and teasing behaviour not enjoyed by the recipient. By labelling comments as 'harmless banter', (predominantly) men expect to be excused of their inappropriate and unwanted comments and behaviour. Sometimes these exchanges are equal and welcomed, and sometimes they are not. For me, these experiences happened a long time ago, but reflecting on them now, I realise how masculine that environment was and how intimidating it may have been for some clients (especially women, or those who did not 'fit' with the hegemonic masculine ideal). This led me to consider if women clients, or *tattooees*, were experiencing this, then what were the women *tattooers* experiencing in this same environment?

Although research on tattoo and gender has been approached in terms of tattooed women as consumers, there is a notable lack of focus upon women tattooers – placing women in a position of passive consumer rather than active producer. Research has also neglected to explore how women and gender relations have influenced the tattoo industry. Although the complexities of the industry in terms of internal relations and dynamics have been, in some ways, investigated in terms of hierarchies, this is often not through a gendered lens. I anticipated that using gender as a lens through which to explore the tattoo industry would offer a valuable insight into a heavily masculinised culture and how women and queer artists manage, negotiate and resist this. I have also become increasingly aware – and in awe – of the changes women and queer artists are making to the industry, and I wanted to explore, document and celebrate these changes throughout this book.

Ladies Who Tattoo: A Potted History

The historical narrative of tattooing in the West is anchored in well-rehearsed and somewhat over-used rhetoric surrounding romanticised tales of sailors and criminals. Women have been largely written out of tattooing history, despite their integral role in the cultural development of tattooing in the West (Braunberger, 2000:4). Although I do not aim to offer a full history of women tattoo artists here, I want to not only contextualise and situate this book but offer space and respect to the women who paved the way for so many others. By considering a selection of artists and their experiences, we can begin to explore and highlight the (in) consistencies between women tattoo artists' experiences of the past and of their experiences today.

Women like Betty Broadbent and Artoria Gibbons are notorious in tattoo history for their connections with travelling circuses and carnivals of the late nineteenth century and early twentieth century. The carnivals often featured 'freak shows' and side-shows, showcasing individuals thought of as 'oddities' at the time, including heavily tattooed men and women (Thompson, 2015:23). By the 1920s, hundreds of tattooed men and women were employed in circus side-shows, although the women performers proved more popular than their male colleagues, with their revealing clothing and their often 'exotic' and erotised stories of how they came to be so heavily tattooed (Thompson 2015:24–25). Stories were fantastical, often centring around the tattooed female body of the reprimanded woman who once enjoyed 'too much' freedom and paid the price for it (Braunberger, 2000:9). Interestingly, however, these stories did not reflect the reality of these women's lives. Women lived off money earned through their tattooed bodies, and this often-meant increased independence and money, as well as more opportunity for travel than would have been the norm for women of this time (Braunberger, 2000:10). For the women watching in the audience, these 'tattooed ladies' represented a fantasy of freedom that they themselves perhaps never fulfiled – the freedom to choose their own pathways in life and to have autonomy over their bodies (Thompson, 2015:25).

The first reported woman tattoo artist was Maud Stevens, a circus performer in the United States, who became Maud Wagner after marrying her tattooist husband, Gus Wagner, in the early 1900s (Mifflin, 2013:31). Maud and Gus worked together for years, although Maud was listed in advertisements as 'M. Stevens. Wagner', to appease those clients who were not happy to be tattooed by a woman (Osterud, 2009:26). Britain's first woman tattooist was Jessie Knight, who began tattooing in 1921 and remained Britain's only female tattooist for decades (Mifflin, 2013:36). In 1955, Knight came second in the 'Champion Tattoo Artist of All England' contest (Iqbal, 2017) and her family believed that it was being a woman that prevented her from being awarded first place.

By the 1970s, the number of women tattooists had not increased significantly, although the number of women getting tattooed had started to rise. Sheila May, who worked in her husband's shop in 1966, only knew of one other woman artist, and said that it took over 10 years to hear about other women in the trade (Mifflin, 2013:55). In 1972, Vyvyn Lazonga began an apprenticeship in the United States with Danny Danzi and eventually became an influential woman in the field – not only for her artistry but for her status as a heavily tattooed woman. She had full sleeves in the early 1970s, which was unusual at the time, especially for a woman, and she won 'Most beautifully tattooed woman in the world' at the 1978 World Tattoo Convention (Mifflin, 2013:57). Despite her prestige, however, Lazonga still endured prejudice from male artists, who disregarded her at conventions on the premise that women should not be *that* tattooed. This is an early illustration of the double standards women had to, and still must, endure: gaining respect and prestige for being tattooed, but so easily crossing the line of what is deemed acceptable by both the mainstream and the subculture. Lazonga resisted the criticism; she opened her own shop in 1979 and is still a renowned artist in the field today.

Ruth Marten, a New-York based self-taught artist who began tattooing in 1972, avoided much of the sexism experienced by Lazonga by working from a private studio at home. Tattooing had been illegal in New York since 1961, and so a private studio was also crucial in avoiding prosecution. In 1977, Marten completed art school before becoming a tattooist, which was unusual at the time (Osterud, 2009:30). She had planned a project to bridge the gap between fine art and tattooing, by tattooing famous pieces of art onto art collectors' skin (Mifflin, 2013:60). This was an innovative idea, and although it did not take off at the time, it is not as unusual in today's tattoo culture, and maps the beginnings of tattoos association with the world of fine art.

Jacci Gresham, another important woman in tattoo history, was the first well-known African-American artist in 1976 and remained the only prominent woman of colour artist, reporting that she did not meet any other women of colour in the industry until the 1990s. Gresham's tattooist husband taught her how to tattoo, although ironically (and further to Lazonga's experiences), he imposed a ban on tattooing women in their shop due to the social unacceptability of tattooed women. Gresham, however, abolished the ban and continued to tattoo women (Mifflin, 2013:66).

It is important to acknowledge this vast historical background of women in tattoos, and to challenge the notion that tattooing has and was something done by men, to men. Although centuries apart, parallels can be drawn between the tattooed ladies of the circus side-shows, and the women tattooers of today. The negotiation of femininities and challenging the boundaries of social acceptability, at the same time as using tattoo as a vehicle for independence, can be mapped throughout the history of women and tattoos from the nineteenth century to the present, highlighting frequently occurring issues surrounding sexism, prejudice and male dominance, which brings us to the point at which my research began. Mifflin suggests, 'For a new generation, the barriers to the profession have been cleared' (2013:107), but is this really the case?

Women Who Tattoo: My Research

There has been a sharp rise in women tattoo artists (and women tattoo consumers) since the 2000s, and the visibility on social media (such as Instagram) suggests that in terms of numbers of women artists, the field *appears* more equal. I want to explore whether the actual experiences of women artists correspond with the suggested shift in the composition of the industry. Women appear to be represented in terms of numbers, but how is the industry responding to this change? How also, are women attempting to change the industry, and perhaps offer something different to what the tattoo community has been accustomed to. Much of these changes have been the result of negotiations made by artists in their attempt to find space within the industry, and these negotiations were a central theme in the artists' narratives.

> Domination explains the ways in which women are oppressed and either accommodate or resist, while negotiation describes the ways women and men bargain for privileges and resources.
>
> (Gerson and Peiss, 1985:322)

As this quote illustrates, negotiation entails a set of interrelated discussions or subtle and often invisible compromises. My research exposes these, along with the conflict and contradiction that often comes with negotiation. I explore what these negotiations mean for the women on a day-to-day basis, and the paradox, complexity and ambivalence that accompany these day-to-day experiences.

Thompson (2015) states that 'The experiences of women within the industry are important to consider, as they will be at the forefront of changes within it' (2015:123), and, therefore, this book focuses on the *effect* women and queer artists have and are having on the industry, as well as their experiences of it – through interviews and conversations with artists, I not only explore tattooists as producers of sub-cultural artefacts and alternative art, but as producers, activists and agents of change and progress. DeMello described the tattoo community as having undergone a 'middle-class turn' (DeMello, 2000:43). I argue now that tattooing has been undergoing another cultural shift – not only effected by the shift in class but also by the shift in gendered influence within the community – a *gender turn* – and this turn sees women, non-binary and queer artists intervening, interrupting and disrupting the traditionally masculine tattoo culture.

My research sits within the field of subcultural studies, whilst contributing to discussions surrounding alternative femininities, emotional and aesthetic labour, conformity and resistance. Although tattooing in the West, as a trade, has its roots within and across subcultures, the level of professionalism required means that this subcultural practice intersects the mainstream field of bodywork and employment, which offers another alternative lens through which to consider subcultural traditions and leads to my exploration of the *sub-cultural* space as a *work*space and place of employment.

Feminist Methodologies: My Methodologies – **Or What I Did and Why**

Although debates about what constitutes feminist research are varied and vast, feminist researchers begin with a political commitment to 'produc[ing] useful knowledge that will make a difference to women's lives through social and individual change' (Letherby, 2003:4). 'Feminist research practice' is recognised as distinguishable from other forms of research, with focus on the questions asked, the position of the researcher within the process of the research, the intended purpose of the work produced and the political and ethical issues raised throughout the research process (Letherby, 2003:5; Maynard, 1994:14). Influential factors and key characteristics of feminist research include: women's voices to be brought to the forefront; reducing or eliminating exploitation; women not being treated as objects for the benefit of the research; and that the research contributes towards reducing the conditions of oppression (Letherby, 2003; Maynard, 1994; Ramazanoglu and Holland, 2002; Skeggs, 2001). The political nature of feminist research, and its potential to bring about change, is, however, potentially problematic – is research that does not bring about political change, therefore, not feminist? (Glucksmann, 1994). And how as researchers, do we know if the research has brought about change, especially for the individuals involved in the research? Feminist research enables us to 'reflect on and attend to dynamics of power, knowledge, relationships, and context throughout the research process' (Ackerly and True, 2020:2) and as a feminist, it is important for me to acknowledge my attempts to adhere to this research ethic.

I wanted my research to focus upon women's experiences and how women make sense of these experiences. I do not strive to expose the 'reality' of the tattoo industry, and this is not something I would claim possible for this book. Instead, I centre the experiences of the participants (who often have their experiences decentred by the industry they work in), whilst exploring and interrogating the differences and ambivalence in the narratives. These contradictions can become an integral part of the research and should not be considered a drawback or potential problem. I value and appreciate the subjective experiences of the participants, and their accounts of these experiences, and hope that my discussions reflect this. I cannot and would not speak for all women, all women tattoo artists or all of my participants and understand that this research is a brief glimpse into the experiences of a very small proportion of women, non-binary and queer people in the industry. As Holland (2004) suggests, rather than creating and constructing a universal body of truth, research provides an opportunity to discover what is important to the people interviewed (2004:4–5). All too often, women's voices, opinions and experiences are devalued and belittled, leaving many people feeling as though they are alone in many of their experiences. By collating these voices, feminist research can, in some ways, validate individual experiences and go some way to assure women and queer folk that they are, in fact, not alone and their experiences matter. My research offers an invaluable snapshot of an industry grappling with contemporary issues surrounding gender, identity and the role of work in shaping and understanding the lives of the people at the heart of the sub-culture.

Reflexivity and Theorised Subjectivity: Making the Researcher Visible

It is important for feminist researchers to place ourselves within the research, acknowledging what we bring to the research and the effect we have upon it. Knowledge production is not a one-way street, and it is, therefore, also important to acknowledge the impact that conducting research has *upon us*. During the research, I became increasingly aware of the prejudices I had been socialised into throughout my involvement with the tattoo industry. Spending time in traditional, male-run studios meant my knowledge of the tattoo industry was shaped by 'old-school' male tattooers who favoured apprenticeships as a way of learning the trade, and consistently conjured a 'good' vs 'bad' tattoo binary. As I became more involved in my research, I could recognise my own personal bias and prejudice with regard to what constitutes a 'good' or 'bad' tattoo and artist, and now my views have changed significantly, and I have the research participants to thank for this. This illustrates not only the importance of reflecting upon the research process, but it also provides insight into the perils of being an insider in the research field. My initial views were very much influenced by me being involved in tattoo culture, and this was a challenge for me as a researcher.

Reflexivity is an important aspect of feminist research – being open about why and how we do research, our bias, and the effect this has upon the knowledge produced, allows others who read the work to understand the circumstances in which the research was conducted and produced. Holland (2018) talks about the presence of love within her research, and I too would like to acknowledge this here. Academic work doesn't often discuss the love and emotion that may have driven it, and yet so often a love for what we are writing about is a strong motivator behind what we do (Holland, 2018:11). As Holland (2018) suggests, 'emotion is missing generally in accounts of sociological research' (2018:80), and I believe there is value in acknowledging the emotional attachment and response we, as researchers, will feel throughout the research process. Participants are also likely to have an emotional involvement in, or attachment to, the research, and thus construct their own ideas about the researcher and the purpose of the research, and this will shape how they present themselves and their narratives. The artists' love for tattoo and tattooing was evident throughout the interviews, and this was not only interesting to hear but humbling to witness and an important part of the research. By providing an insight into our personal investment and motives behind the research – for both the reader and the participants – we can work towards developing and embracing a feminist methodology.

Positionality and recognition of this is key in any feminist research project (Deutsch, 2004; Dinçer, 2019), and as a cis white woman I experience the privileges that come with this, which is important to acknowledge. I wanted my research to be as intersectional as possible, acknowledging the important interplay between gender and other identity factors such as race, sexuality and class. And although I have focused upon the relationship between gender and tattooing by interviewing women, non-binary and queer artists, I had hoped that my sample of participants would be more diverse in terms of race and ethnicity. However, having relied on artists coming to me voluntarily in the first phase of interviews, I had no control over who would or would not volunteer – most of the artists who volunteered were white, with the exception of LC.

LC was the only person in the first phase of interviews to mention race and tattooing; interestingly more of the participants spoke about race in the second phase of interviews – perhaps indicating that, years later, the industry is getting better at recognising the problem of racial inequalities within it. The fact that race was not an initial recurring theme within the data tells us something important about tattoo culture and illustrates the overarching whiteness of the tattoo industry – something that requires further academic attention. It also illustrates that as a researcher it is important to note what is not said, as well as what is. Sometimes, non-recurring themes are just as relevant and important as those that are recurring. LC was surprised when I told her she was the only interviewee to talk about race (in the first phase of interviews), which illustrates the need for a more diverse research sample. I was torn between interviewing the women who came to me voluntarily, whoever they might be, or purposefully seeking out possible participants because they were women of colour. My decision to focus on the women who volunteered means my sample was narrower than I had hoped. Research carried out by a woman of colour may have attracted a more diverse set of participants and I would be very excited to read any research that built upon my own! For the second phase of interviews, I did contact several artists of colour, but they either did not respond, or didn't want to take part. Talking to more women of colour would have, I am sure, identified further underlying issues within the industry – specifically surrounding how women of colour experience the hegemonic masculinity and inherent whiteness of the industry. Although there are relatively high numbers of Black Women getting tattooed, these numbers are not matched with Black Women becoming artists (Mifflin, 2013:120) and often leaves women of colour feeling like 'outsiders in an industry comprised of out-siders' (Mifflin, 2013:120). Artists already established in the community speak of the lack of Black Women in the industry and the difficulties they have had in finding apprenticeships and studios to employ them (Mifflin, 2013:120–1). Although Mifflin's research offers a brief look at the barriers faced by women of colour in the industry, it is not an in-depth exploration of the racial inequalities within tattoo culture, and this, it appears, is something lacking within academic research on tattoos and tattooing. Other research on race and racism in tattooing includes work focusing on the appropriation of tribal bodily practices by contemporary Western culture (Pitts, 2003), and although there have been an increasing number of media articles focusing upon cultural appropriation of *tattoo imagery* (Coles, 2016; Richards, 2015), academic research is yet to fully address current discussions. This opens opportunities for further research, and I feel research on the intersectional inequalities of tattoo culture would be a rele-vant and important extension of this project.

My Methods

I spoke to 20 artists in total, 18 of whom identified as women, one identified as non-binary and one as gender-queer. I wanted the interviews to be semi-structured, utilising a more conversational exchange, and initiated this by using three open-ended questions:

(1) Why tattooing?
(2) What are your experiences of being a woman, non-binary and/or queer in the industry and the tattoo subculture?
(3) What are your experiences of being tattooed? Both inside and outside of the sub-culture.

I conducted the interviews in two phases – most of the interviews were con-ducted in the first phase; the second phase of interviews happened 5 years after the first and enabled me to re-interview two of the original participants, but also focus on artists involved in the #tattoometoo movement which had occurred since I conducted the first interviews.

It was impossible, geographically, to even consider interviewing some of the artists face-to-face. In the initial phase of interviewing, the artists who'd agreed to speak to me were based in Australia, the United States and the United Kingdom. I gave the participants a choice of possible interview methods, and conducted some via Skype messenger, one face-to-face and the remainder were email interviews – all by choice of the artists. The interviews I conducted later, were all via Zoom – something that post-lockdown (during the COVID-19 pandemic), didn't seem as strange as when I had arranged the Skype interviews years before.

To begin creating interest in the project, and gathering names for my research sample, I used Twitter as a digital-snow-balling tool, akin to the more traditional 'word of mouth' snowballing method used previously by social researchers. Most responses were from customers giving me the name of their artist, often including comments on the artist's capabilities as tattooists, and sometimes comments on the artist's character or personality (for example, 'she's lovely') which shows the emotional involvement and level of attachment some artists nurture within the client/artist relationship. These responses also illustrate how clients might display their sub-cultural capital and knowledge of the industry.

Emails were generally exchanged over a period of around 3–4 months (although some were longer due to a delay in responding) and most interviews consisted of 3–4 lengthy email exchanges. Conversations often felt informal; some interviewees asked me for my opinion on certain topics, or referred to me being tattooed and presumed I would understand or empathise with the point they were making – identifying and highlighting a common ground.

I used Instagram more and more as time went on. I followed certain artists (mostly women and queer artists) and tattoo accounts, so that I could keep up to date with not only the artists' work but the work they were doing to share knowledge and raise awareness of toxic behaviour and sexual misconduct in the industry. I contacted my second group of interviewees via direct message on Instagram, which worked well. When it was time to analyse the data, I used thematic coding to categorise the recurring themes from the interviews. Due to the small size of my sample, I coded the data manually. This not only suited the amount of data I was working with, but I found manual coding aided my connection with the data, enabling a good working relationship with the narratives of each participant, the themes and any limitations that arose. I have used initials when quoting the participants in the book – these initials were chosen at random by me and bear no relation to the artists' actual initials. This is purely to maintain anonymity throughout the discussions and is common practice in feminist and sociological research. As most of the interviews were conducted via email, the responses were typed by the participants – I have not edited the responses and so quotes remain how they were originally written by the participants.

Email interviewing worked well for both me as the researcher and the participants. Interviewing via email gives the participants power in choosing when and where to respond. Writing responses may also give the participant more power and control over their narratives, giving them time to reflect on the questions and consider their responses (James, 2016). Face-to-face interviewing lends itself to building rapport with interviewees, but it is still possible to build rapport via email interviews. Holland highlights how important it is that 'data is participant-led, that subjective issues and experiences are allowed and given space' (Holland, 2018:20). This, for me, not only relates to the content of the interviews but the way in which the interviews are conducted – email interviewing allowed the participants the space and thought needed to reflect on their experiences, building their responses in a constructive and discursive manner. I also liked that writing emails was reminiscent of letter writing as a feminist research method (Letherby and Zdrodowski, 1995), and this was reflected in a response from IK:

> Looking forward to it [the interview] - you've engaged my other passion - letter writing, haha, so you can expect some long ones back.
>
> IK

Whilst I was carrying out my fieldwork, I was invited to be interviewed by somebody who was conducting research for their undergraduate degree. This was a useful exercise for me – not only was I able to reflect upon how interviews have the potential to reproduce identities through constructing a narrative in the interview, but I was also able to reflect upon how my participants may have felt during the interview process. My interview was also conducted via email, and I appreciated having the time to consider my answers. I know I would not have given the answers I gave if I had been interviewed face-to-face. This is not to say I embellished or constructed answers that were not true, but having the time and space to think about my experiences and remember details was useful, and I think my interview was richer and deeper because of this.

The benefits of an email interview may be enjoyed by the interviewer too, and at the time of the research, as a working mum conducting research part-time, interviewing via email worked well for me. I could spend time planning my responses, ensuring I asked the questions I needed to ask and was not put under the pressure of a face-to-face interview. There is also the issue of transcription – with email interviews; the transcription is of course already complete. So when fellow researchers lamented at how time consuming and laborious transcribing was, or I read researchers accounts of their dislike of the transcription process (LeBlanc, 1999:29), I felt a little like I had cheated when I sheepishly told them I had conducted email interviews and, therefore, had avoided the dreaded task.

The second phase of interviews all conducted via Zoom, again, through the artists' choice. I wonder if the effect of the pandemic and our reliance on online platforms had an impact on the artists' choice. Western society became so familiar, reliant and confident with platforms such as Zoom that opting for those over email perhaps felt like the natural thing to do, post-lockdown. These interviews, with consent of the participant, were recorded and then unlike the first phase, required transcription – which was a stark reminder of how lucky I was to have avoided this in the first phase!

Of course, interviewing via email or video-call does rely on the participants having access to the internet and being IT savvy. This would exclude some potential participants from taking part in the research, and I would hope that any researcher would offer an alternative method of interviewing to anybody who wanted to take part but could not do so online. Another disadvantage to emailing is the difficulty in participating in emotion work in some instances. For example, one participant told me (via email) about a group of men engaging in highly sexualised, harassing behaviour whilst she tattooed one of them. This came as a shock to read and my reaction was that I wanted to support, empathise and talk to the respondent about the experience. I felt that I could not offer immediate empathy and when I wrote back, I referred to the incident, but felt my response lacked the emotion it would have had if we had been face-to-face.

Fieldwork was an exciting time in the research. Receiving emails from participants made me feel humble and grateful, and I was always eager to read the responses. I found myself reading through each response at speed, excited to learn more about each respondent. I then took time to read through again, probably two or three times (if not more), to digest the data, begin to analyse and write my response and further questions, tailored to each participant's responses. The luxury of having time to plan my response was a huge benefit of email interviews. One of the disadvantages to consider was the pressure I felt to keep up the momentum with correspondence. It was important for me to reply in a certain time-frame so that the participants felt they were appreciated, and being heard, but also because if I allowed the correspondence to lag, there was a risk that the participants would also.

Sharing thoughts and experiences did not seem to be difficult for many of the interviewees – being a tattooed person and having to think about your body, and answer multiple questions about your body and choices made about your body (often daily!), means that many of the women had already spent time in their lives contemplating their position within the industry and were aware of their feelings towards their positionality, role and attitudes. Women who have experienced sexism in the industry will often have processed this privately (just as any woman experiencing sexism in the workplace or elsewhere), attempting to 'make sense' of it without the prompt of being interviewed about it. I think previous self-reflection probably aided the research process and meant the participants could draw upon these reflections within their responses. It did not seem 'unnatural' for many of the women to be working through and reflecting upon their experiences, many of them not only describing their experiences but beginning to analyse them also.

Power Relations in the Research Process

The need to address an imbalance of power between researcher and participant is central to any feminist research project. There are ways of reducing this imbalance, such as informed consent, ensuring the participant has the option of leaving the process at any time, and being open and honest about the aims of the project. However, is it possible to eradicate the unequal power relations completely? And are the 'unequal' power relations as simple as this researcher/participant binary viewpoint might suggest?

Power in the research relationship can often be fluid in nature, and it is wrong to assume that the researcher continually holds the power in comparison to the 'powerless' participant. The fluctuating power dynamic between myself and the artists I spoke to became increasingly evident throughout our exchanges and seemed to be in constant flux. I made sure to provide a brief biography of myself – including that I am tattooed and had previously worked in a tattoo studio. This was important in breaking down some of the obvious power imbalances between myself and the participants; I would not expect a participant to share information with me without knowing a little bit about me first, and I felt it important that they know I am tattooed and, therefore, an 'insider' to the community. Developing a non-hierarchical relationship during the research process is important to feminist research and sharing some information about myself went a little way in achieving this.

Our emails were friendly, open and informal. Many of our email exchanges ended with the artist asking if their answers were 'ok' or what I 'needed' – this may have been to ensure the sender has 'done the right thing', but I also think these responses illustrate the nature of the exchange and how the artists felt about the interaction. Not only did they want to 'help' and be helpful – which suggests an almost instant emotional attachment to the research project – but it felt in some ways as though they wanted to check that they were providing the right answers. At the same time, I also felt that this desire to 'help' also placed the participants in a position of power – they hold the information that I need to carry out my research, and, therefore, by sharing this information with me, they are *helping me out*, and thus, more powerful than I in the research process; this further illustrates the complex power relations at play during the feminist interview process. My responses to the emails I received were also personal and somewhat emotional – on looking back over the email exchanges, I found myself apologising for being a potential 'nuisance' to one participant, to which she replied,

> You aren't a nuisance and I am happy to answer your questions.
>
> This is also helping me to sort out where I want to be and what I like/dislike about the world of tattooing.
>
> I hope this helps.
>
>   NT

I think it is somewhat of a default position of a feminist researcher to feel a degree of guilt for taking up somebody's time and feeling as though you are 'putting them out' in a lot of ways; expressing this in the emails and apologising for it is, I suppose, an attempt to acknowledge this for the benefit of the participant, and for one's own 'peace of mind'. NT's response is also an illustration of how the research can at times benefit the participant, and highlights some of the limitations of literature which describes the researcher and participant relationship as one of exploitation of the latter by the former.

There were instances during the interviews where a participant might inform me of resources or information that I was not previously aware of and although as a researcher I may hold power within the research process and interview exchange, yet in terms of sub-cultural capital, the artists I interviewed hold more capital than I do. I found myself feeling an element of self-doubt arise during the fieldwork; I started to question where I fit into the subculture, and, of course, how the interviewees would view me – maybe not as an insider at all.

Using a feminist methodology can (or should?) enable the collaborative potential of the feminist interview process. I had been contemplating whether to bring feminism into the research in a direct way, for instance, ask the participants if they identified as feminist and probe whether this affected the way in which they worked. However, I was hesitant to do so, and I have since reflected on why this was; I think that, as a feminist, I am so aware of 'feminism' being a 'dirty word' in many circles that I did not want to jeopardise the relationship with the participants. I wanted to ensure I maintained a rapport – and perhaps mentioning the dreaded F word, risked disrupting the interactions between the participants and me. That said, my main motivation for conducting the research was my feminism and looking back at this hesitation, I realise just how contradictory my thinking was. How could I come to the research via my feminist politics, and yet be worried about being open about my feminism? I also realise how this contradicts my aims for a feminist methodology – on the one hand, I empathise with feminist researchers' attempts to be open and honest about our place in the research, and yet, on the other hand, I was keeping my main motivations from the participants to keep rapport and get 'good' data. Talking about my tattoos may have been an easy task, but talking about my feminism, however, was apparently not! When, therefore, LC described growing up in a punk feminist community, and explained that she identified as feminist, this gave me 'permission' to be explicit about my feminism and I was able to thank LC for this.

Industry, Community and a Sub-cultural Field: A Note on Terminology

Whilst I aim to avoid the distraction of an in-depth debate around the nuanced terminology and definitions of subculture, I do need to clarify the terms I have chosen to use for the purpose of my research. As my work focuses largely on the artists themselves, it is especially important that I can clearly differentiate between tattoo collectors as a generalised group, and tattoo artists as an interdependent but distinct collective.

The tattooed community has never been a homogenous group and with the appropriation and popularisation of tattooing through popular culture, I feel it would be inaccurate and unhelpful to use the term *subculture* to describe it. It has become more difficult to show resistance through style and symbols due to the blurring of boundaries between what is deemed 'alternative' and what is deemed 'mainstream' (Muggleton, 2000). However, tattooing as an aesthetic practice is still used by members of many subcultures to display subversive style and acts of resistance or affiliation. In his research, Atkinson describes meeting 'riot grrrls, goths and psychobillies' who all used tattoos to demonstrate their sub-cultural membership and subsequent 'dislocation' from mainstream culture (Atkinson, 2003:99). Tattooed people do not constitute a subculture, but tattooing as a practice intersects numerous subcultures and, therefore, is what I would call, *trans-subcultural*. The formation of the tattooed community means that there are sub-communities within the bigger tattooed collective, and there are subcultures which transcend the tattooed collective. The collective is fluid and transient, rather than fixed and easily definable.

The tattoo artists, being the trans-subcultural practitioners within the tattoo community, form a distinct but interconnected group within the community. My research will show that although artists should not be deemed a subculture per se, as a group they undoubtedly display subcultural-like attributes whilst working in the tattoo *industry*. To explore the relationships, hierarchies and other subcultural-like aspects, I need to retain a link with the term subculture and with subcultural theory. I, therefore, propose that tattoo artists constitute and operate within a *sub-cultural field*. The introduction of the hyphen retains the link with subculture as a structural and theoretical term, at the same time as denoting a collective that if not a subculture of its own, is certainly sub-cultural in many ways and is certainly on the peripheries of mainstream culture. It also allows me to use subcultural theory on some levels, to analyse the aspects that *do* mirror a sub-culture, but at the same time, provide a distinct marker to illustrate the degree of separation between the terms. I will also, therefore, use the term *sub-cultural capital* with the addition of the hyphen to indicate capital that has transferred, or transfers between the mainstream and sub-culture, meaning it is no longer specifically *subcultural* but yet retains some elements of being counter-cultural. *Sub-cultural capital*, therefore, describes the capital that fluctuates between, and permeates, both the mainstream and the sub-culture, yet strives to retain its subcultural-like status, namely to preserve 'authenticity'. I will also continue to use *subcultural capital*, without the hyphen, when referring to capital present exclusively within subcultures.

I have chosen to use the term *community* to describe the collective of tattooed people in which the artists work. In her ethnography, *Bodies of Inscription*, DeMello (2000) explores the creation of a community around the appreciation of tattoos. DeMello explains that although the term community could refer to any tattooed person, she uses the term to mean those tattooed people who 'actively embrace the notion of community and who pursue community-orientated activities (like attending tattoo shows)' (2000:3). She acknowledges that although the tattoo community is open to all tattooed people, it is indeed hierarchical and is largely defined by elite tattoo artists and middle-class tattoo magazine publishers (DeMello, 2000:3). DeMello admits that community is a contested term in relation to the tattoo collective, and that it may hide the significant variation and conflict within the tattoo culture; indeed, within the community there are many over-lapping, intertwining groups and sub-communities (DeMello, 2000:3). DeMello recognises that the group is not homogenous, and there is a hierarchical nature to the internal relations of the community, but her work focuses upon how the community itself is defined, constructed and maintained. As Atkinson (2003) states, the tattooed collective may not be one homogeneous group, but having and getting tattoos does mean you share something with other tattooed individuals, and it provides a talking point (Atkinson, 2003:109). Therefore, for the purposes of my research, I will use community to describe the collective of tattooed people. Although it may be a community that is transient and fluid, with members opting in and out of involvement over time, I would argue that in certain contexts (studios and conventions, for example), there is certainly a sense of community that being tattooed can offer.

Chapter Outline

Chapter 2 will highlight relevant themes and discussions from empirical research on subcultures and tattooing – with gender as a focus – to enable us to centre women and girls in the research. Research on tattooing and class highlights the shift in how tattoos are being accepted into mainstream culture and the paradox this creates for many members of the tattoo community, with the middle-class appropriation we have seen. I look specifically at the role, position and experiences of women in subcultures, highlighting the similarities between and across previous research and illustrating the recurring issues that arise for women and girls in alternative subcultures. Although initially, different subcultures may appear to be unrelated to tattoo culture, music and sport cultures present similar issues surrounding the negotiation of femininity and gender, hierarchies and capital.

Chapter 3 is the first of the analysis chapters, and it is here that I begin to explore women tattoo artists' experiences of a both male-dominated and overly masculinised industry. I examine how women have navigated the transitions from subcultural consumer to sub-cultural producer and subsequently, how they have negotiated their post-transition space within the tattoo industry. The data brings to light questions surrounding who holds capital, who is deemed authentic, and how capital is legitimised. Whilst considering the nuanced experiences of the artists and the conflicts that arose within and across their narratives, a range of paradoxes emerged.

Problematising these paradoxes encouraged me to consider how the imagined experiences of subcultural employment compared to the lived reality of working in a highly-masculinised sub-cultural field. I use *male-dominated* and *highly-masculinised* as two distinct terms, because the industry is both male-dominated in terms of numbers of men artists, but also highly-masculinised in the way in which it produces and reproduces certain 'masculine' norms.

Chapter 4 develops and extends the discussions surrounding femininity, examining how some of the participants spoke about utilising their femininity in a more positive way than the management of femininity we saw in Chapter 3. I consider the employment of feminine and female capital and how the women use, experience and make sense of this in their role as tattooers in tattoo studios as a workplace. I identify and introduce conflicts between displaying signs of dominant versions of femininity, and utilising the traits associated with these dominant femininities – exploring the artist's opinions around using femininity in appropriate or acceptable ways – and their critique of artists who cross these boundaries. Focusing on body work and the emotional and aesthetic labour attached to work on the body, I interlink gendered capital and emotional labour, along with notions of aesthetic labour and the tattooed body as a symbol of professionalism. I also consider the pressures that this brings in terms of performativity and how artists navigate this in relation to clients, and mainstream attitudes towards them as artists. The chapter asks questions around how gendered capital has the potential to disrupt the masculinised culture of the industry.

Chapter 5 builds upon previous chapters, developing further the idea of resistance within the industry. I explore how women, non-binary and queer tattoo artists are doing and thinking about tattooing differently: intervening, interrupting, and disrupting the masculine culture of the industry. I ask what effect this is having upon the industry, and the community. The chapter also explores the contradictions in resistance, outlining the conflict and ambivalence that arises when a subcultural participant is not only resisting the mainstream, but elements of the subculture also. This chapter explores the #tattoometoo movement and how women, non-binary and queer artists are attempting to change the industry, making a safer space not only for them, but their clients too.

Chapter 6 draws upon the key concepts, paradoxes and conflicts discussed throughout the book, and collates, summarises and concludes the key findings of the research. This, for me, was the most difficult chapter to write. I became increasingly aware of the need to do justice to the participants and their stories and felt panicked at the thought of misinterpreting their experiences. Subcultural capital, gendered capital and femininity are all concepts further problematised, in order to identify how my research contributes to conversations about alternative femininities, counterculture and the complex and contradictory interrelations of differing forms of capital.

Women have a long history in the world of tattooing, although their stories and experiences are fragmented through and within the sub-culture itself. My research aims to create a space in which to centre women's, non-binary and queer folks' experiences whilst exploring the nuances, paradoxes and complexities that being a minority artist in the tattoo industry brings. My research will bring women out of the circus side-show and consider what it means to place them at the centre rather than on the peripheries of an influential sub-culture.

Chapter 2

Gender, Subcultures and Tattooing: Bringing Women to the Front

Women circulate as signs but are not theorised as sign producers.
(Russo, 1997:328)

It is well-documented that women and girls have been largely ignored by much of the early research on subcultures (McRobbie, 1991, 1994). Women and girls were likely to be placed on the peripheries of any exploration of subcultures – in a position of silent by-stander or girlfriend to the active male participant. It is not only important, therefore, that girls and women are written into subcultural research, but equally important that they are researched as subcultural *authors* and credited for the roles they play in the *creation* of community and culture, rather than just the consumption of it. In her research into girls in punk, LeBlanc (1999) argues that researchers often depict girls as 'passive victims of female socialisation' and 'dupes of the cultural forces that degrade them' (1999:13). Through my work in this book, I seek to address this trend, and centre women as active producers and participants of the tattoo sub-culture.

Subcultures are often seen as vehicles through which members resist dominant norms and structures; historically, however, there has been a deep-rooted connection between subcultures and dominant ideologies of masculinity, and subcultures are yet to successfully challenge the dominant boundaries of gender inequalities (Brill, 2007). Very often, alternative subcultures are male-dominated and typically 'masculine' in their presentation, traits and practices, and, therefore, the way in which subcultures are experienced is very different for men and women, boys and girls, and anyone identifying as non-binary or queer. This means that not only do subcultures often harbour sexist and misogynistic attitudes, but homophobia is also a systematic problem (Ambrosch, 2016).

Subcultures centred around alternative music, (some) sports and art networks are contexts in which women often find the opportunity to challenge conventional femininities (Finley, 2010:365; Holland, 2004; Kelly et al., 2005, 2006; Klein, 1997; LeBlanc, 1999; Messerschmidt, 2002; Moore, 2007; Mullaney, 2007; Wilkins, 2004). However, unlike the male participants of a subculture, women must contend not just with dominant, mainstream culture, but also the patriarchal structures replicated within the subculture itself (Evans and Thornton, 1989:17;

Tattooing and the Gender Turn, 17–31
Copyright © 2023 Emma Beckett
Published under exclusive licence by Emerald Publishing Limited
doi:10.1108/978-1-80262-301-720231002

Holland, 2004:23). Looking at women in subcultural sport such as skateboarding raised themes similar to those in my own research; and although sport may seem to hold very few similarities to the world of tattooing, the subcultural characteristics, the hegemonic masculinities and the effect these have upon the women within the subcultures show significant parallels to my own work. Women-led subcultures such as roller derby and riot grrrl, discussed further below, offer insights into alternative versions of femininities, resistance and the creation of women-only spaces – all of which are themes developed in my own discussions throughout the book. Although the tattoo industry is not a subculture per se, its structural workings and characteristics in terms of capital and hierarchy mean it is important to explore the collective as a structure of some kind, with agents acting *within* it but not necessarily always *independently* of it and, therefore, research on subcultures provides useful analytical and theoretical tools through which to explore the intricacies of the tattoo industry as a community and structural body.

'Youth' subcultures have been an important part of sociological research (Hall and Jefferson, 1993), but subcultures and subcultural lifestyles are not reserved for the young, and this, like gender, has been largely ignored throughout empirical research. Early feminist writers including McRobbie (1991, 1993), Lees (1993), and Thornton (1995) worked on redressing the balance by researching girls in subcultures, but there remains a lack of research on the continuing practices and participation of adult women (Holland, 2004:24). Exploring the voices of women tattooists adds valuable insight to existing work on the experiences of 'alternative' adult women and their negotiation of various subcultures, dispelling the myth that people adopting any kind of 'alternative' lifestyle or aesthetic will merely 'grow out of it' eventually.

It is also important to highlight here that my research explores the experiences of women who not only pursue subcultural *leisure* activities, but who also construct careers within the subculture itself – influencing the *construction* and *reconstruction* of the culture. We must examine and highlight how women are resisting the sexist frameworks and structures so pervasive within and across subcultures. With a focus on active participation, authorship and resistance, this chapter contextualises my own work by bringing women to the front of research on subcultures, whilst highlighting common and relevant themes from the research on tattooing.

Subcultural Women: Resistant Women

I want to acknowledge the Riot Grrrl movement here, and how influential it has been not only on me personally, but on many women who affiliate with alternative subcultures. When conducting my fieldwork, I was often reminded of a riot grrrl ethic – whether it be in the ethos or attitude of the artists I was interviewing, or the Do-it-Yourself (DIY) activism they were involved in. The Riot Grrrl movement began in 1991, emerging from the punk and independent music communities of Olympia and Washington, DC. 'Riot grrrl encouraged women and girls to take control of the means of cultural production' (Schilt, 2004:115). Girls became producers of their own music and zines, with a focus upon their own subjective experiences (Pavlidis, 2012:167). Riot grrrl began as a women-led alternative to the 'violent and misogynist tendencies growing within the punk scene at the time' (Pavlidis, 2012:167–8). Women actively resisted hegemonic subcultural norms that historically positioned women as silent bystanders. Resistance was gained by appropriating traditionally male roles, as well as tackling issues around gender and sexuality through the disruptive positioning of their bodies – through music performances, conventions and gigs (Piano, 2003: 258). The Riot Grrrl movement, based on politics and activism, helped shift women's position within punk from consumer/observer to that of producer – enabling and encouraging women's resistance, involvement in subcultural feminist networks and the creation of spaces for feminist cultural production (Piano, 2003:254). The movement saw women sustaining their resistance to men's dominance by controlling the production, distribution and promotion of their creative activities (Garrison, 2000; Klein, 1997; Moore, 2007; Mullaney, 2007). There are important links to be made here with women in tattooing and how, in more recent years, with the increase in women in the industry, women-run studios and artist-managed social media accounts – women artists too are controlling the production, distribution and promotion of their creative output.

During my research, it became apparent that the numbers of tattoo zines and blogs published were increasing, and that many of these were created and managed by women – which again are reminiscent of the Riot Grrrl movement and ethos. When I started to get tattooed, the internet was not as easily accessible and, therefore, I relied on magazines for my sub-cultural knowledge. Magazines were only available from the top shelf of a small number of newsagents and were not as culturally rich or diverse in representation as some are now. Most magazines available throughout the 1990s and 2000s featured covers with minimally-dressed women who, apart from being tattooed, conformed to society's perception of what a woman *should look like* in terms of body shape, further alienating many tattooed women and exacerbating the feeling of not belonging to the subculture. Although not exclusively *for* women, blogs such as *Inkluded* (now disbanded) were created because the author felt like she didn't belong in the traditional tattoo community. Various in-print zines were, and still are, created to tackle and discuss the sexist attitudes towards tattooed women. *Things and Ink* magazine was created by author Alice Snape who wanted to create a magazine that celebrated female tattoo culture and provided an alternative to the more traditional tattoo magazines I mentioned above. The first in-print edition of the magazine was published in 2012 and although it is no longer available as a physical magazine, the blog continues online, embracing an artistic and inclusive approach to tattoo journalism. This desire to create a different space for women to share their experiences and ideas began to shift the dynamic of the tattoo culture – and paved the way for activism such as the #tattoometoo movement discussed in Chapter 5. This changing sub-cultural landscape shows the shift within the tattoo community, towards greater acknowledgement of the sexism and hegemonic masculinity experienced by so many people and is a direct result of action taken by women to highlight and disrupt the hegemony within the sub-culture. The ability to 'talk back' (hooks, 1989) means women can talk about, address and challenge dominant and subcultural discourses, raising questions about normalised inequalities and increasing opportunity for resistance and change (Piano, 2003:258–9). It is important as researchers to shine a light on the way women strategise resistance, and to acknowledge that although resistance is often situated by subcultural studies between conflicting (and false) binaries of conforming to the dominant order (LeBlanc, 1999:17) – what exists in reality is a complex set of negotiations and compromises.

Tattooed Women: Negotiating Femininities

As numbers of tattooed women in the West increased throughout the 1990s and 2000s, there was a surge in academic research focusing upon women and body modification, situated within a wider context of feminist debate surrounding the body in both feminist theory and activism (Pitts, 2003:10). The notion of the 'body project' was developed by sociologists as a concept framing the body as something to be worked upon, explored and transformed as part of an individual's self-identity and mode of self-expression (Pitts, 2003:11; Shilling, 1993). Feminist scholars have focused upon a variety of body projects, including dieting (Bordo, 1993, 1997; Morris, 2019), cosmetic surgery (Bonell et al., 2021; Davis, 1995, 1997; Gimlin, 2006) and bodybuilding (Hockin-Boyers et al., 2020; Marshall et al., 2019; Monaghan, 1999). Tattoos were embraced by some feminists as body projects that subverted traditional notions of 'feminine beauty', enabling women to regain control over their bodies (Pitts, 2003:55). The long-standing concern surrounding control over women's bodies has been central to feminist thought (Morgan, 1991; Pitts, 1998), and tattoos were, therefore, beginning to be framed as a welcome alternative to body projects that maintained and upheld societal norms and expectations around the 'feminine' body. Body modifications such as piercing and tattoos not only challenge conventional beauty norms but have the potential to subvert mainstream ideals – challenging normative hegemonic constructions of a passive femininity and 'beauty myths' (Craighead, 2011:43; Wolf, 1990), in turn providing opportunity for a 'revolutionary aesthetic for women' (Braunberger, 2000:3), as well as offering the opportunity for women to 'reclaim' their bodies after physical or symbolic victimisation (Atkinson, 2002:225; Pitts, 2003:15; Thompson, 2015:39–41). Body modifications are replete with cultural messages about conformity and resistance, and this is illustrated through the nuances seen in the analysis of women and body modification (Atkinson, 2002:230).

It is important to acknowledge that tattooing and the tattooed do not exist in isolation from each other or mainstream culture and society. Interactions with the mainstream public play an important part in consolidating a subculture, establishing its boundaries and compelling its members' commitment and so if we are to gain a better understanding of tattoo culture, we must explore the dynamics of the relationships within and outside of the community, as well as the influencing factors affecting these relationships. Research has found that in some contexts, tattoos *reproduce* established ideas around femininity and the feminine body, rather than subverting or challenging them. Women who, therefore, choose tattoos as a vehicle for subversion find themselves balancing resistance and conformity, leading to fluctuating feelings of 'angry defiance and careful negotiation' (Holland, 2004:139). The location and placement of a tattoo on the female body and the size of the tattoo chosen does have an impact on the way the tattoo is 'seen' or 'read' and may, therefore, reproduce dominant feminine norms rather than challenge them – women will often take this into consideration when choosing their tattoo (Atkinson, 2002:226; Dann, 2021:75). Women who use tattoo as aesthetic adornment, rather than a subversive practice, often remain aware that tattooing the 'wrong' part of the body or having the 'wrong' design could result in the body being read as purposefully deviant by mainstream society (Atkinson, 2002; Dann, 2021:90), in relation to social norms and expectations surrounding 'acceptable' versus 'unacceptable' femininities (Dann, 2021; Gerson and Peiss, 1985:321).

If we add motherhood into the discussion surrounding the tattooed female body, we see yet another layer of how women's bodies and femininity are policed. Dann and Callaghan (2017) explore the 'complex construction of the tattooed female body, as interwoven with the role of mother' (2017:10) – further developing the discussion surrounding the 'right' and 'wrong' way to be tattooed. The tattooed mothers interviewed created an 'us and them' division between what they thought to be acceptable tattooing and unacceptable – playing on classist stereotypes of the working-class woman, whose tattoos are 'too loud or obvious' (Dann and Callaghan, 2017:14). Discussions also centred on authenticity – having tattoos that 'mean something' being seen as more acceptable than tattoos that didn't 'mean' anything (Dann and Callaghan, 2017:10). 'Meaningful tattoos' can also be linked to a middle-class narrative that is well thought-out and rehearsed, making tattoos more 'acceptable' to the middle-class sensibilities, and legitimised by middle-class cultural capital (Demello, 2000). Being a tattooed woman and embodying what it means to be a tattooed woman brings a complex series of presumptive norms and values to navigate. Negotiations of femininity are, therefore, paramount in any discussions around women and the tattooed body – women often develop 'stocks of knowledge' relating to other people's attitudes towards tattooed women and need to incorporate these into their rehearsed and anticipated social interactions with strangers (Thompson, 2015:155).

Compromise is a tactic used by many women when they are dealing with the tensions between subverting traditional notions of femininity and having to adhere, at times, to societal norms and ideals. Changing clothes, taking piercings out, covering up tattoos or styling their hair differently to usual are all examples of the compromises women might make. Women very quickly become accustomed to the unwritten 'rules' around when it is and is not appropriate to push the boundaries of dress and appearance and will adhere to these when needed (Dann, 2021:51–2; Holland, 2004:89). In her book, *Alternative Femininities* (2004), Holland interviews a participant who kept her work identity and home identity purposefully separate, not only wearing different clothes, but storing them separately at home to create a distance between her work self and 'real-life' self. Some of Holland's other participants, in comparison, had found or created jobs that allowed them to be their 'true selves', meaning they dressed how they wanted to dress, made no sacrifices or compromises around their appearance, did not have to 'tone down' their look and felt lucky that they were able to do this (Holland, 2004:91–2). Building upon this, my work explores whether women working in an alternative industry avoid this need for separate work identities, and whether the tattoo industry provides a space for artists to truly 'be themselves'.

The relationship and interaction between subcultural women and the mainstream, along with the negotiations at play, also highlights how boundaries are created and maintained by women *within* the culture as well as outside of it. Holland's participants discursively located their own femininities as different to mainstream versions of femininities by, for example, using the term 'girly' with negative connotation. The women talked about conventional femininities as being oppressive and restrictive, so that their own femininities might appear more positive, creative and 'free' (Holland, 2004:143). Holland identifies this as a 'recuperative strategy', which allowed the women to present their own femininities in opposition to dominant norms of femininity, and at the same time frame these alternative femininities as desirable rather than 'other' (Holland, 2004:144). Holland also identifies 'flashing femininity' as another strategy (Holland, 2004: 144). The women, when fearing their alternative appearance eroded certain 'feminine' aesthetics, would also use items associated with more traditional femininity to recuperate their feminine identity (Holland, 2004:144). The participants spoke about their use of traditional feminine items such as perfume and make-up, false eyelashes or carrying a 'feminine' handbag, to 'reassure' others that they were indeed feminine, 'despite' their outward appearance suggesting otherwise (Holland, 2004:46).

It appeared important for many of Holland's participants to feel both alternative and different, and yet feminine and womanly at the same time. They did not want to be one or the other and were keen to express this. Their resistance was not always a resistance to being feminine, but a resistance to 'culturally bound ideas of traditional femininity' (Holland, 2004:146). There was a tension between their alternative selves and their desire to be feminine, but at the same time, not wanting to be considered 'girly' (Holland, 2004:146). Holland describes a paradox evident in the narratives, which seemed to be linked to ageing, between the participants wanting to be alternative and 'out there' but also wanting to avoid feeling judged (about being 'too old' to be alternative, perhaps) and, therefore, vulnerable at the same time (Holland, 2004:124). As Holland suggests, femininity is still reliant upon and defined by constraint, and the appearances of alternative women are often not 'restrained', signalling disdain for traditional femininity and mainstream rules, norms and ideals (Holland, 2004:46). However, there is a paradox between the lack of restraint that the alternative appearance portrays, and the control, care, time and effort that goes into producing and creating an alternative look. Therefore, an 'alternative' identity does not necessarily 'free' women from the time-consuming rituals associated with traditional 'beauty' regimes (Holland, 2004:46). Negotiating between 'acceptable' femininities within and outside the subculture does not necessarily mean women transform the unequal dynamics between masculinity and femininity (Finley, 2010:366); unconventional femininities do not always hold the resistive power required to challenge deep-rooted ideals of masculinity and femininity. How do women produce new 'femininities' in negotiation with hegemonic femininities without reproducing hegemonic gender relations between masculinity and femininity? (Finley, 2010:366), and how does (or can) this relate to women's role within the tattoo industry?

My research sets out to explore how women negotiate their femininities within a male-dominated sphere, and will ask what, if any, compromises are made by the artists themselves. When women appear strong or powerful in comparison to displaying more stereotypically feminine traits such as being small and weak, women take up more 'space', and are more visible. This can threaten the normative order of gendered spaces and sometimes women are faced with negotiating and appeasing interactions within these spaces (Holland, 2004:99). This was an important consideration throughout my research – how are women who are 'taking up space' in a masculinised industry and threatening the gendered norms of the culture received by the industry? Women tattoo artists are often (but not always) heavily tattooed, and therefore 'visible'; they are also taking on the role traditionally associated with their male colleagues – are there consequences to this, and if so, what are they and how do women artists manage them?

Gender, Seriousness and Authenticity

A lack of women-dominated subcultures means girls and women who want to reject the hegemonic expectations and norms of mainstream femininity sometimes turn to masculinised subcultures to enable them to adopt an alternative set of rules around feminine identities (LeBlanc, 1999:142). However, due to male domination, subcultures often develop masculine normative standards (LeBlanc, 1999:106); women often find themselves having to 'fit in' and exist amongst those standards, negotiating between masculinities and femininities in both the main-stream and the subculture. Constraints of 'masculinised subcultures' often mean that women's forms of gender resistance 'are tempered by the accommodations they make to the masculinity and male domination of their chosen surroundings' (1999:226). Male-dominated subcultures often support masculine identification in boys and men while challenging feminine identification in girls and women, meaning the process of gender construction within subcultures is very different for girls, boys and non-binary folk (LeBlanc, 1999:105). Culture seen as 'overly' feminine, or associated with girls and women, is often devalued as 'imitative and passive' in comparison to masculinised culture which is deemed more worthy (Thornton, 1995:105). Therefore, women in subcultures often find themselves fighting to be accepted by both mainstream society, whereby they are negotiating levels of 'acceptable' femininity, and the often male-dominated subcultures, where being a girl or woman means they are not taken seriously.

Due to the masculine nature and gendered structure of many alternative subcultures, male knowledge is often considered authentic and legitimate, whilst girls and women are faced with a questioning of their knowledge and position within the subculture – often being asked to 'prove' themselves and justify their subcultural membership. Men are often regarded as knowledgeable 'experts' within a field, whereas women have to 'work' hard at gaining the same level of respect and authenticity and may not ever be considered as authentic as men. It seems, therefore, that although subcultures are presumed to reject mainstream norms and ideals, they often, in fact, replicate and reinforce the structural inequalities present within wider society. Research on subcultures has found that although alternative communities might claim to be inclusive and active in their quest for equality, women are often outnumbered by men, and felt that the culture was inherently hyper-masculine – leading to women feeling unwelcome and unimportant as members of the scene (Haenfler, 2004:428). Research into heavy metal music subcultures shows that women who *played* heavy metal were afforded more capital than women who did not, but were, however, still compared to male musicians (Nordstrom and Herz, 2013). Women were consistently compared to men's presumed authenticity, and rather than being judged on their own merit were judged against men's skills and termed 'not bad for a girl' (Nordstrom and Herz, 2013:464). This also highlights the similarities between capital in and amongst subcultures and the dynamics of how this capital operates. Women may hold more capital if they are active producers of the subculture, but they are continuously ranked against the credentials and authenticity of the men producers of the subculture – contributing to the almost constant battle for recognition and respect.

Maddie Breeze's work on Roller Derby (2013, 2015) provides a vital and insightful analysis of how femininities and gender relate to negotiations of seriousness and authenticity (2013:2–5) – developing the idea that authenticity and legitimisation is heavily gendered which is something I discuss in further detail in Chapter 3. Roller derby typically opposes the dominant discourses of sport, which leads to a struggle for power and authenticity in the field of *mainstream* sport, but it is also seen predominantly as a 'woman's sport' and, therefore, becomes a site of gender contestation, which amplifies the struggle for power, authenticity and seriousness (Breeze, 2015:22). Breeze introduces the idea of a 'feminine apologetic', whereby an emphasis on dominant and 'conventional feminine attractiveness' is utilised as an 'apology' for the transgression into the masculinised field of sport (Wughalter, 1978:12, in Breeze, 2015:23) – this builds upon the discussions above and is of particular relevance to the tattoo narratives throughout this book, further highlighting issues surrounding compromise, compensating and negotiation.

Better Than 'Them': Capital and Hierarchies

Capital is a central theme throughout this book and became a useful tool through which to make sense of the artists' narratives. Although capital is perhaps commonly associated with money, wealth and assets, and although financial capital and earning a living is paramount in the world of tattooing, the most significant and influential type of capital to tattooers and their clients is not monetary. It is apparent as soon as one enters the sub-culture that one's position in it depends upon the *sub-cultural capital* earned. From working in, and spending leisure time in and around tattoo studios, I have seen how individuals are treated differently on the grounds of their capital, or lack of. Some are ignored, scoffed at and disregarded, whereas others are celebrated and treated with respect. It became apparent that subcultural capital, gendered capital and the appropriation of capital by the mainstream were dominant themes in terms of how capital manifests in the tattoo industry, and it made for an interesting thread to explore.

Subcultural capital can be, according to Thornton (1995), objectified or embodied (1995:11). Objectified capital is described as artefacts such as books and art or even haircuts, something that can be displayed to demonstrate capital. Embodied subcultural capital is, for example, using language specific to the subculture to demonstrate being 'in the know' (Thornton, 1995:11). Subcultural capital can be seen as the 'linchpin' of an alternative hierarchy, displaying *authentic* and *legitimate* knowledge inside and outside of the subculture (Thornton, 1995:3). This leads to a construction of an 'us' and 'them' and creates the 'imagined other' (Thornton, 1995:101) – this is not only a hugely significant concept when considering subcultural capital and how it 'works' within a given subculture, but it is also a recurrent theme in recent research on tattoos and tattooing (see Dann, 2021; Lane, 2021) – further highlighting just how pervasive the division is. Although members of any given (sub) culture may not constitute a homogenous group, they are often happy to identify a homogenous crowd that they *do not* belong in – this both establishes their own position within their chosen subculture and contributes to the feeling of community and sense of shared identity (Thornton, 1995:111). The construction of the 'other' and how this relates to sub-cultural capital was something I highlighted during my fieldwork and will be discussed in more detail in subsequent chapters – who is the 'other' and what purpose do they serve in the narratives of the artists? What constitutes subcultural capital in the tattooing field? How do artists gain subcultural capital and what does that capital look like/consist of?

Jensen (2006) argues that not only is it important to understand subcultural capital within subcultures, but we need also to understand how capital relates to outside socio-structural differences and forms of power. This would increase the understanding around positions of power inside and outside of the subculture by exploring the intersections between class, gender, ethnicity and race of the participants and the capital they are afforded within the subculture (Jensen, 2006: 265). In linking this to possible sexism, racism and homophobia within subcultures, we could further interrogate who is awarded capital, who is not and why – and ask if discrimination plays any part in this. There is such fluidity between and across the mainstream and the counter-culture of tattoo that considering power and how it relates to outside socio-structural differences is paramount.

Another key premise in the work on capital is the idea that it is only useful if it can be successfully converted into other types of capital (Jensen, 2006:268); for example, Thornton explores the conversion of subcultural capital into economic capital, and argues that although it does not convert as easily as perhaps *cultural* capital does, there are financial rewards for the possession of subcultural capital in some subcultures (Thornton, 1995:12). In her own research, Thornton uses the examples of DJs, club organisers and music journalists, to illustrate members of the subculture who hold a significant level of subcultural capital, and who successfully convert this into economic capital. Thornton suggests that individuals who gain economic capital from working in a subculture not only gain respect through their high volume of subcultural capital, but also through their role in defining and creating the culture (Thornton, 1995:12). This, however, is very much dependent upon levels of subcultural capital awarded and held, and throughout the following chapters, I explore the complex and nuanced relationship between subcultural capital, gendered capital and economic capital of artists within the industry.

It is not only artists who benefit or are impacted by sub-cultural capital, and it is important to highlight here that the tattoo community as a whole is built upon hierarchies, maintained and sustained by the possession of sub-cultural capital. Scholars have identified *elite collectors* (Irwin, 2003; Lane, 2021; Thompson, 2015) to be members of the community who have extensive coverage and 'desire the best art available' (Irwin, 2003:29). Collectors will travel far and wide to visit the artists they desire 'work' from, and often have 'wish lists' of tattoos they desire from specific artists. This group of 'elite' collectors has grown significantly over the last two decades – perhaps due to the increase in artists, the quality of the tattoos by a larger number of artists, more widespread circulation of information about artists through social media and tattoo media and the rise in tattoo conventions – meaning more movement between international artists. Instagram has been very influential in the progression and development of tattoo culture (Barron, 2017), creating a virtual tattoo scene that has not only adapted styles of tattooing, but has had a huge impact on tattoo collecting and the sharing of knowledge and information (Force, 2022:420). The change in attitudes towards tattoos in western society, and the lessening of the stigma attached to body art, may also be a factor in the rise in popularity and increase in people with extensive coverage. Collectors and artists, however, often see the popularisation of tattoos as threatening tattoo's 'fringe status' and with that, a threat to the sub-culture too (Irwin, 2003:38). Being part of something that was once marginal but is increasing in popularity within the mainstream is problematic for some who have chosen to express their non-mainstream beliefs and attitudes and is something explored further in the following chapters of this book.

Mainstreaming Capital: A Paradox

For the tattoo industry, and the sub-culture, the 'mainstreaming' of tattoo as an aesthetic practice has had a complex and nuanced effect upon the community and the people within it. As well as non or new subcultural members gaining knowledge of the sub-culture from outside sources, subcultural capital can be marketed to large numbers of consumers outside of the sub-culture who want to appear associated with the sub-culture, or to be following the latest fashions

(Moore, 2005:232). This can be seen not only in the celebritisation of tattoo (Dann, 2021:16), but also in the use of tattooed models in mainstream advertising campaigns, and tattoo imagery used in non-tattoo related marketing and design. The boundaries between subculture and mass culture are often more fluid than subcultural participants believe. Often, when style, music or other distinguishing markers of the subculture are marketed in the mainstream, subcultural members 'experience a sense of alienation because they no longer own or control the culture they have produced, and their expressions of rebellion are now consumed by the "mainstream" audience they define themselves against' (Moore, 2005:233). One notable and influential factor in the mainstreaming of tattooing is the rise in tattoo-related television shows.

There has, since the 2000s, been a variety of TV shows focusing on differing elements of the world of tattooing – they usually take one of two different approaches. The first being reality-type shows based in various tattoo studios and the second, focusing on people who regret their tattoo choices, have made seemingly 'bad' decisions, and need them 'fixing' (Dann, 2021:33). There is usually a 'funny' or humiliating story to tell about the bad choices made, encouraging the viewer to laugh or mock the tattooee, the questionable tattoo design is then covered by another artist with a bigger, 'better' design.

Tattoo reality shows, on the other hand, gained huge popularity in the early 2000s – with *Miami Ink* being the first to be aired in 2005. *LA Ink* followed in 2007 and after that came several spin-offs of the same TV formula (Thompson, 2019:303). These shows brought tattooing into the everyday lives of people who hadn't had any contact or association with tattooing previously and had a significant impact on the mainstreaming of tattooing (Thompson, 2019:303). The narratives in the shows were often that of a confessional nature, or of tattoos being chosen for self-help purposes and showed the client sharing their 'story' behind their choices – usually warranting a degree of sympathy from the viewer, and very much relating to the middle-class narratives discussed above. The effect of these shows has been met with varying reactions from artists and people within the community, and was something discussed during my fieldwork, revealing mixed and slightly contradicting feelings surrounding tattoo knowledge being shared with mainstream culture.

Chapter 3 explores how the dissemination of subcultural capital to the mainstream impacts upon the artists' capital within and outside of the sub-culture. Subcultural insiders' identities depend upon an opposition to the mainstream and, therefore, commercialisation of the subculture can lead to feelings of a loss of identity (Moore, 2005:233). Members of a subculture who embrace commercial exposure to increase their own commercial success are often accused of 'selling out' (Moore, 2005:233). It is also vital, therefore, for the subcultural participants to distinguish between insiders of the subculture and the outsiders who appropriate the subculture's symbols and artefacts. This ability to distinguish between the two also serves to 'validate one's claims to autonomy and authenticity' (Moore, 2005:245). Subcultural participants who identify with a subculture to demonstrate their resistance to the mainstream and consumer ideals are faced with the same mainstream consumer culture claiming the subcultural style and artefacts as *their own*. The ability to distinguish between who is authentic and who is not serves also, therefore, as a defence against this appropriation and lack of authenticity (Moore, 2005:249) – and is further evidence that an 'us and them' binary is a consistent and persistent concern for members of the community.

When subcultures and the mainstream intersect, a complex set of relations is established between members of the subculture and members of the mainstream who adopt the aesthetic, style and symbols of the subculture. When tattoo knowledge seeps into the mainstream, the relationship between the alternative, the mainstream and capital is complexified, especially for tattoo artists. The relationship between subcultures and the mainstream is further complicated if members of the subculture benefit from a positive relationship with the mainstream. What happens when subcultures want, to some extent, to be considered legitimate and authentic by mainstream culture, but at the same time want to remain on the peripheries? This is something explored further in the subsequent chapters.

Shifting Class Dynamics

One of the most notable changes throughout the history of Anglo-American tattooing is the shift from what was once a working-class trade to a profession built upon skill, artistry and middle-class sensibilities. The 'middle-class turn', as DeMello describes it (2000:43), has had an influence on various factors within the tattooing sub-culture, including the increase in women getting tattooed and the 'artification'[1] of tattooing as a practice. Before attitudes towards tattooing in the West started to change in the 1960s, the world of tattooing was reserved mainly for working-class men, both in terms of the clientele and the tattooist. Skills were gained through an apprenticeship with an established tattooist, and they were more likely to be motivated by economic gain, rather than the desire to produce highly aesthetic pieces of art. In contrast to the world of tattoo today, there was little association with the more traditional art world (Sanders, 1989:18). This class shift became a central focus for academics exploring tattoo culture; research spanning the 1980s, 1990s and 2000s highlights the effect that the middle-class turn has had upon tattooing.

The route into tattooing has, like the community itself, changed significantly over time. Traditionally, tattooists would learn the trade through a mentor and apprenticeships. The apprentice system was a successful way of reproducing skills and techniques, while at the same time ensuring only a certain amount of people were entering the trade (Adams, 2012:157; Lane, 2021:76). The use of apprenticeships was (and still is) used as a way of gatekeeping who does and does not enter the industry – which, as we will see in the following chapters, can create significant barriers for lots of artists. There are ways of avoiding these barriers, although they are not seen by many established artists as favourable ways of

[1]Artification is a term generally used to describe the transformation of non-art into art (Kosut, 2013:3) and is discussed in more depth later in the chapter.

entering the industry (Lane, 2021:85). Teaching yourself is, although not always successful, an option and is made even easier now with YouTube video tutorials and 'tattooing kits' being sold on websites such as eBay, and the more recent addition of 'tattoo schools' (Lane, 2021:84) available online or in person.

There is often a divide and a hierarchy between artists who have learnt tattooing in the more traditional way, and those who have self-taught. The term 'scratcher' is synonymous with the tattoo community and is used in a derogatory fashion to denote someone who perhaps lacks formal training or skill (Lane, 2021: 21). It acts as a rhetorical social distancing tool for those artists who have entered the industry via apprenticeships or mentoring and serves as yet another way of constructing an 'other' to distance themselves from.

Along with self-taught artists and *how* people enter the industry, the other significant transformation within the industry is *who* enters it. The tattoo industry, in the United Kingdom and United States, has increasingly become more aligned with the more traditional worlds of art (Lane, 2021; Lodder, 2022). The shift from a working-class trade to one more focused upon aesthetics and artistic ability is thought by scholars to have been due to the influx of younger tattooists with art-school backgrounds who became interested in tattooing as a form of expression, and an alternative medium for their art (DeMello, 2000; Sanders, 1989:19). The rise in tattooists with fine art degrees brought a new aesthetic and set of skills to the industry; although young people had always been attracted to the culture, the new tattooists were coming to work with knowledge of art theory and a desire to transform tattooing (DeMello, 2000:84; Lane, 2021). For some academy-trained artists, choosing to tattoo to support themselves was a more favourable option than trying to enter the over-saturated and often impenetrable contemporary art world (Kosut, 2013:9). This was evident in some of the narratives within my own research, and may be of specific relevance to women artists, who may find that like so many other creative industries, the art world holds fewer opportunities for them than their male colleagues (De Montfort et al., 2016); tattooing as a career may offer more opportunities and appear to be an achievable alternative. However, as the following chapters will explore, now that the tattoo industry is becoming saturated with artists, perhaps competition between artists and a struggle for authenticity within the mainstream means that tattooing does *not* provide women with an alternative to the art world at all.

For some, making efforts to align with the art world brings legitimacy, respect and financial reward, although this may be met with resistance from other artists within the industry. The artification of tattoo reveals a literal and symbolic change in the medium of tattooing (Kosut, 2013:4; Lodder, 2022). It is not uncommon for today's tattooists to produce art in other mediums such as oil, acrylic and watercolour and much of this artwork is displayed in studios, and in some cases, in specialist exhibitions in traditional art galleries. During the COVID-19 pandemic and national lockdowns, producing art and art prints was one of the only ways for tattooers to make money whilst studios were closed. These artists have bridged the gap between the art world and tattoo culture by conceptualising the two realms as extensions of each other rather than as polar opposites (DiMaggio, 1987; Kosut, 2013:13). As a group, the new generation of tattoo artists have been quite successful in redefining tattoo culture from inside of the field – terms such as 'tattoo art' rather than 'tattoo', and the classification of 'tattoo artists' rather than 'tattooist', are commonly used throughout the contemporary sub-culture and provide evidence that fine art ideologies and practices have been widely integrated and accepted (Kosut, 2013:14). However, the cultural status of tattoo remains in flux outside of the tattoo community. Many of society's non-tattooed mainstream still 'read' tattoos in the context of its marginalised and deviant reputation (Dann, 2018). At the same time, certain cultural gatekeepers have begun to popularise and elevate tattoo via exhibitions and shows at cultural institutions, meaning that as a cultural form, tattoo hovers between high, low and popular culture, depending upon the tattoo itself and the context in which it is produced and displayed (Kosut, 2013:3; Lane, 2021:125).

The shift in class dynamics has not only impacted the tattooer and tattooing as a profession, but the tattooee also. Class very much intersects with gender, as highlighted in the work of Dann (2021). Tattoos once seen as a marker of the working-class have been somewhat gentrified by the middle classes who, by using 'smaller, daintier, pretty tattoos in specific locations has allowed them to be a part of the tattooed community, and use the mystery of a tattoo for their own aesthetic' (Dann, 2021:7). Middle-class labelling of tattoos as 'art' makes this form of once working-class body modification more acceptable. Tattoos can be seen to transgress class boundaries, at the same time as reproducing them (Dann, 2021:87). As discussed above, in Dann and Callaghan's (2017) work on tattooed mothers, this very much intersects with the 'right' and 'wrong' place/design/size of tattoo chosen, and the reading of the feminine and masculine body of the wearer. In Chapter 1, I noted that the tattoos I grew up surrounded by were very different from the tattoo culture I know today; I now recognise that what I was noticing was this class distinction. My family's tattoos were very much a working-class aesthetic. Whereas the culture I later became familiar with was the result of the middle-class appropriation of that very same culture.

Conclusion

Research shows that women consistently have to prove themselves, their knowledge and their authenticity within the subculture – whatever the subculture. Pitted against male subcultural participants, women must 'earn' their place and are constantly tested by members of the subculture who hold more capital and are deemed more authentic. Research on roller derby differs slightly in that it is a culture dominated by women; however, issues of ambivalent investments in seriousness, authenticity and legitimacy explored through a gendered lens were integral to the development of my own analysis and will be utilised throughout the subsequent chapters.

The dynamics of the tattoo industry as a sub-culture differ in some ways from many of the subcultures researched previously, due to its leisure/employment status. Many of the subcultures studied previously are embedded within leisure pursuits and industries. Although getting tattooed is itself a leisure activity, my research focuses upon tattooing as *employment* and this, therefore, adds another intersection through which to explore the interrelations of the sub-culture. Research has been conducted on occupational and organisational subcultures (Trice, 1993), but these also differ from the tattoo industry as this research focuses upon subcultures *within* organisations or employment fields, whereas the tattoo industry *is* the sub-culture at the centre of my exploration. This provides a unique standpoint from which to explore tattooing, sub-cultures and labour.

Subcultural relationships with the mainstream are complex and nuanced and whilst considering previous research, and during my own analysis, it became evident how vital it is to acknowledge, interrogate and problematise the fluidity of these relationships between mainstream and subculture. Discussions on subcultural relations with the mainstream include notions of resistance, agency and conformity along with mainstream appropriation of subcultural artefacts and the idea that subcultures are at risk of 'selling out'. This fluid and sometimes contradictory relationship is often accompanied by feelings of ambivalence in subcultural members, and by utilising previous research, I can interrogate the paradoxes within my own research narratives, identifying the ambivalence expressed by the participants. Subcultural socialisation is thought to be a predominant factor in how the cultural values and norms of the subculture are maintained (Wicks and Grandy, 2007:351) and my work explores the role of *gender* in socialisation, asking whether socialisation into the tattoo subculture different for women. And if so, what effect this might have upon their position within the industry.

It is important that we, as researchers, explore notions of resistance through the ways in which subcultural members construct *their own* resistance depending upon the context, not just how the subculture itself resists dominant culture (Haenfler, 2004:408). The tattoo community may or may not be resisting mainstream culture at any given time, but what became apparent in my own work was women artists resisting elements of the industry, from within. What it is that the women are resisting? What does this resistance look like? How does the resistance affect women's position within the industry, and what happens when we broaden our understanding of resistance, to consider not just the sub-culture's resistance to the mainstream, but also forms of resistance *within* the sub-culture itself?

Chapter 3

Being a Sub-cultural Professional

Central to many of the artists' narratives around their choice of tattooing as a career was the idea that tattooing allowed them to 'be themselves'. This, however, was not the narrative of all the women, and I began to question, *who* feels they can be themselves, who does not and why? The narratives highlighted issues surrounding authenticity and legitimacy, underpinned by the notion of subcultural capital and what it means to be a professional within a sub-cultural field. Who holds capital? What is deemed to be authentic? And how is this capital and authenticity legitimised? This chapter explores how women have navigated a transition from subcultural consumer to sub-cultural producer and subsequently how they have negotiated their post-transition space within the tattoo industry. By exploring the nuanced experiences of the artists and the conflicts that arose within and across their narratives, I start to examine how the imagined experiences of subcultural employment compare to the lived reality of working in a male-dominated sub-cultural field.

From Consumer to Producer: Tattooee to Tattooer

For many of the women I interviewed, their connection with alternative lifestyles and subcultures was an important part of both their identity and of their pathway into tattooing as a career. Through exploring and understanding this commitment and devotion to their alternative identities, I wanted to understand how a career that allowed these identities to be experienced in a professional setting was so important to them.

> I knew younger than 14 that I would be an artist, as drawing and painting were my all-time favourite things to do. I was fascinated by tattoos, I was also really into music, and the punk movement (OK, I may have been a few years too late, but I loved it all the same ...). It all fit so well. ...
>
> YA

> I never fit in at school... So as I got older, I dyed my hair crazy colours, I played guitar, and got piercings. I wore expressive

Tattooing and the Gender Turn, 33–57
Copyright © 2023 Emma Beckett
Published under exclusive licence by Emerald Publishing Limited
doi:10.1108/978-1-80262-301-720231003

makeup and alternative clothes. When I was old enough I got tattoos. I didn't want to fit in anymore and having my body art said to the world, 'I'm not average'. ...

After 5 years of getting tattooed and harassing every tattooist I came into contact with, I managed to get a traditional apprenticeship at [a studio] in Birmingham. This is [tattoo artist's] old shop, so has a great history.

KB

I was always interested in doing tattoos. I would draw in sharpie on my best friends, I grew up in a punk feminist community in Oregon, and all the dykes I loved had tattoos. I was especially fond of tattoos that prevented someone from working a normal job, tattoos that crept up the neck or down the hands.

LC

YA, KB and LC all express an interest in, and connection with, non-mainstream, non-conforming cultures. Punk subculture, body piercings, dyed hair and tattoos are all used as symbolic indicators of living a lifestyle that does not necessarily conform to what we might term 'the mainstream' and is what Pitts (2003) terms 'symbolic rebellion' – creating a subcultural style through using already stigmatised symbols such as tattoos (2003:5). KB made the decision to purposefully engage in body projects and practices that would visibly separate her from the mainstream, something she terms as being 'average'. LC also alludes to this with their fondness for tattoos that, in their words, prevent people from working in 'normal' jobs. KB specifically tells us she did not want to 'fit in' anymore, suggesting a conscious decision to ensure she stood out as 'different' from her peers. KB purposefully engaged in body projects to increase her visibility as a young person and although this may seem to be rather typical teenage rebellion to some, in the context of this book, and in light of the careers the women have pursued, the impact of this 'rebellion' has far greater consequence and it becomes crucial to their career paths.

Much of the research on 'youth' cultures fails to acknowledge that many of the young people who are participating in these subcultures continue to engage in some kind of alternative lifestyle as adults. For the artists I interviewed, this was indeed a significant factor in the motives behind their career choices. The connection with alternative lifestyles was not only an important part of their youth, but formative in the identities they embody today. The 'symbolic rebellion' (Pitts, 2003) of tattooing, which was once a practice of personal self-identity and leisure, has become the vehicle allowing the women to be independent adults with careers. These women have not 'grown out' of their alternative lifestyle – they have grown with it and allowed 'it' to grow with them, marking their transition into paid professional work, a symbol of adulthood. During the interviews, many of the artists were eager to express the benefits and opportunities tattooing as a career had afforded them. There are limits to the subversion of societal norms one can engage in within mainstream society, due to the day-to-day constraints put upon individuals to conform (Dann, 2021) and, therefore, if a career can be carved within the subcultures through which this subversion is nurtured, it extends the opportunities to disrupt societal norms.

The ability to 'be myself' was central to many of the interview narratives and included discussions about freedom, power and control. For women like KB, YA and LC, who already embodied an alternative lifestyle and aesthetic, tattooing as a career was said to offer feelings of choice, subjectivity and independence; this appeared throughout the narratives to be a strong influence on their desire to become a tattooer.

> I LOVE my job. I do have the freedom to be exactly who I want to be all day long, and I don't feel many can say that.
>
> AA

> The career path of a tattooist to the 14-year-old me meant I got to be myself: I could wear what I wanted, draw all day, and meet some wicked people along the way! I guess you could say tattooing seemed like a way to express myself and be free [...] I've always been happy to stand out from the crowd, or at least content not blending in. In so many careers I feel you have to conform, or at least put on a 'poker face' for work, you cannot be 100% yourself. But being an artist, I'm almost expected to be a little bit strange!
>
> YA

> I have always been into tattooing because of the sovereignty it affords me. I do very poorly with authority and bosses, and tattooing allows me to run my own business and work for myself.
>
> LC

LC's dislike for authority is, I would argue, a familiar narrative within alternative subcultures and is an important part of LC's sub-cultural identity. LC felt that tattooing as a form of employment provided a solution to having to negotiate authority figures daily within a professional employment context. A career that might enable, encourage and nurture an alternative, subjective identity is likely to be seen as a positive and empowering opportunity for women who are engaging with non-mainstream cultures. It is important to note here that both AA and YA comment on 'other' forms of employment not offering the same opportunities as tattooing in terms of enabling an expression of a true identity and self. Although there were no specific examples of 'other' jobs offered, there was a distinct narrative that alluded to tattooing as being unique in its rewards for the tattoo artist and the maintaining of the self. This suggested that being a tattoo artist does not rely on the need for separate work identities to be constructed in order to succeed, and that being able to 'be yourself' allowed a degree of embodiment of both private and public identities for the artist. 'Other' careers were seen as more restrictive and as requiring a degree of conformity to become successful in the workplace. The ability to be your 'authentic self' (Thompson, 2015) was seen as an important and determining factor in choosing tattooing as a career – as discussed in Chapter 2, so often we are in a position of having to compromise self-expression to fit into our social roles, so working in an environment that not only accepts but creates alternative identities is one very impactful way of reducing the need for compromising self-expression. Thompson (2015) argues that tattooing is one of the most powerful modes of self-expression and is often the one we are required to cover when navigating within and throughout our social roles (Thompson, 2015:112). McDowell's (1997) research on gender and employment also found that the women participants identified their workplace persona as different to their personal persona, having to adopt a 'different sense of myself' and 'not using my real personality' (McDowell, 1997:201); this suggests that compromise is not only felt in an aesthetic sense but also in relation to an emotional identity – this was a significant consideration for many of the artists I spoke to and something I explore further in the following chapters.

LC talks positively about the opportunity for self-employment, introducing the idea that tattooing as a career is not only about identity, creativity and the freedom it enables, but is also a matter of business, industry and production. By becoming tattooists, women who are active members of alternative subcultures – such as the tattoo community – are extending their participation to become active subcultural producers rather than just passive consumers. It is important, therefore, to unpack the issues surrounding this shift and to ask just how easy it is for women to become the authors of the subcultures they have invested so much time and emotion in.

The experiences noted above, however, were not the experiences of every interviewee. If we are to suggest that working within an alternative sub-cultural field such as the tattoo industry gives women the opportunity to avoid and resist mainstream norms and ideals, we must also explore the problems and constraints women may face. Does sub-cultural employment really escape the constraints and restrictions of more mainstream employment? Is the tattoo industry really as welcoming and 'free' as these narratives suggest? What are the constraints, and how do women negotiate them? It may not be as easy for all women in the field to succeed, and it is important that we ask why, through an exploration of the nuanced experiences voiced throughout my interviews. First let's look at apprenticeships – the women I interviewed expressed how difficult it was to get an apprenticeship and some had not been successful at all.

> Initially, I was doing a lot of portraiture for extra cash and absolutely love that, but sadly there's not a lot of demand for that with the economy the way it is. I've always been interested in tattooing and am fascinated by the culture of it all, along with piercing and the fashion aspect too [...] I found it a daunting prospect as the industry can be quite elitist and snobby [...] It was a kind of 'you have to have been born into it to do it' kind of

attitude...[The tattoo industry is] elitist in the sense that when I had approached tattooists (when getting some [tattoos]) about training/apprenticeships/information they were very secretive and not at all forthcoming.

EK

EK was not an active member of the tattoo community before she started tattooing, despite having had some small tattoos herself; and therefore, her route into tattooing differs greatly from that of some of the other artists interviewed. EK came to tattooing as a way of making money and developing her artwork through alternative mediums, wanting to find a space within the field, but finding it difficult to 'break' into the industry. It became apparent throughout the interviews that the route into tattooing, and the background – or habitus – from which the tattooer had 'transitioned' from (i.e. an alternative subculture or fine art) had a significant effect upon how they viewed the industry, how the industry viewed them and how space was negotiated within the field. EK had not accumulated subcultural capital in the way that LC, KB and YA had, and this seems to have had a significant effect upon her opportunity for making the transition from consumer to producer. Even *with* a connection to the tattoo community, as in the case of KB or LC, the narratives throughout the interviews illustrate that it is not easy to get an apprenticeship – words like 'convinced', 'harassed' and 'eventually' were regularly used throughout the interviews, suggesting that there is a lot of work that goes into being 'allowed' to even begin the shift from client to tattooer and, therefore, it is easy to understand the difficulties faced. An apprenticeship is the traditional and most common way of learning to tattoo and if, as I am arguing, the industry has been dominated by men since its formation, most of the tattooers offering apprenticeships have been men. This, in turn, positions experienced male tattooers as the gatekeepers of the sub-cultural field. Without these male tattooers offering and agreeing to take on apprentices, there is little opportunity for women (or anybody) to gain the knowledge and expertise to become, or be 'allowed' to become, a tattooer – and if it is difficult for women to get apprenticeships, we must also acknowledge here that it would be difficult for tattooers from the LGBTQ+ community to find apprenticeships too. Knowledge is authorised and legitimised via the apprenticeship and could be argued to be a 'malestream' method of learning the trade. Anyone who does not learn through an apprenticeship is disregarded and labelled unskilled and not legitimate (Lane, 2021; Wicks and Grandy, 2007:354). Until women and/or queer artists gain a position of power through which to offer apprenticeships of their own, it was and is men who have ultimate control over who occupies space within the industry. Examples of this indirect but effective gatekeeping are seen throughout my interviews, expressed through discussions of tattooing being a 'secret industry'. KB, like EK did previously, also talked about the secret nature of the industry, yet from a completely different perspective.

I guess until quite recently, everything about the tattoo industry was secret. The tattooist was someone who could execute tattoos and no one else knew how to, or could even buy any equipment. Before eBay, and cheap tattoo kits (which the inks in are actually very dangerous) you couldn't get into tattooing without getting into a tattoo shop [...] You didn't know anything about the tattoo industry unless you were getting tattooed.

KB

KB looks back with fondness on a subculture which she has grown up in; to her, the secrecy of the industry was alluring and an influencing factor in her desire to be part of the field. KB, who was affiliated with alternative subcultures before she began tattooing as a career, talks about the industry throughout her interviews using what I would describe as romanticised language, or a nostalgic tone. She talks a lot about how the industry 'used to be', or certainly, how she viewed the industry as a consumer within the community prior to her career as a tattooist. KB developed her interest in tattoos and tattooing during the 1990s, when tattooing was undergoing a shift from its previous associations with criminality, and was becoming more popular with alternative subcultures. KB witnessed the rise in popularity of tattooing, and with this the status and prestige that came with being a tattooer, in a growing community. KB enjoys being part of an alternative culture: it is important to her and she invests a lot of time and emotion in it. This emotional investment has 'paid off' in that she was offered an apprenticeship at a well-respected studio under a well-respected stalwart of the industry. KB already held some degree of capital within the community, accumulated via her affiliation with alternative subcultural aesthetics and could utilise this capital to secure a space in the industry as a prospective professional.

EK, in contrast to KB's experiences, was not an active member of the community and, therefore, had no capital to use in the negotiation of an apprenticeship; ultimately, this had a detrimental effect upon her ability to gain space within the industry. Socialisation is key to maintaining the dominant social structure of the subculture, and (re) affirming the hierarchy and power relations at play (Dupont, 2014:577). Without some level of previously acquired subcultural capital, it seems that breaking through into the field of tattooing is almost impossible.

Subcultural Capital and Industry Hierarchies

It is clear from examining the narratives that holding subcultural capital within the tattoo community plays an important role in women's transition from tattoo consumer to tattoo producer. Capital is a complicated, nuanced issue within both the tattoo community and the industry. Discussions around unequal power relations were dominant in many of the narratives, and it seems that capital and its distribution underpin the negotiation of status, power and hierarchies in the sub-cultural field. Subcultural capital is a way of distributing and negotiating power and is a currency which legitimises the unequal distribution of status within subcultures (Brill, 2007:112). By exploring the nuances of these power relations within individual subcultures we can conceptualise the divisions and hierarchies amongst the subcultural members (Brill, 2007:112). Status was something frequently acknowledged throughout the interviews, and it became apparent that being a tattooer means holding some level of status both inside and outside of the tattooed community. Although this was considered positive by some, and as more negative by others, there was certainly a consensus that this status and prestige existed and was part of everyday life as a tattooer.

Having been an active member of the tattoo community since the late 1990s, I am myself aware of the existence of subcultural capital amongst community members and artists, and have often reflected upon how this capital is awarded and distributed. Capital is nuanced and complex, and it is important to consider who holds capital, who awards capital and whose capital is deemed authentic. The experiences below illustrate how capital works for artists when they engage with those who are outsiders to the industry.

> Some people seriously react almost as if they are meeting a celebrity- it's so absurd- I really do think this is where tattooists can get that ego from, because people really can seem to treat you as though you are special or something. It's good to remember it's just a job like any other!... Most of the time I don't tell people [that I am a tattoo artist] because then I end up having to have incredibly long tedious conversations about it which bore me to tears- countless parties I have been cornered and told about 'this one tatt I have been thinking of for years but I'm not sure if I should get it what do you think...' Ahhh - I find it so frustrating!!
>
> IK

The capital described here is granted by the consumers or potential consumers of tattoos and places the tattooer in a position of status and power. The narratives suggest that capital granted by consumers in this way may be of less significance to artists than sub-cultural capital awarded within the sub-culture itself. Magazine articles, social media representation and endorsement from fellow artists are all good examples of how this sub-capital might manifest. IK explains that she often does not tell people she is a tattoo artist, to avoid long conversations about ideas that may never turn into actual tattoos – IK is managing the disclosure of her identity as a tattooer to avoid the unwanted attention that subcultural capital can bring. Outside the sub-culture, there is a difference, however, between the conversations with people who will never be tattoo customers, and those who are potential customers. It has been argued by academics that some types of capital are only valuable if they can be successfully converted into other types of capital (Jensen, 2006:268) – for example, (sub)cultural into economic. The capital described by IK above, and AA below, is not guaranteed to develop or be converted into anything more than consumer-led sub-cultural capital and, therefore, may not be deemed 'useful' capital.

> Whenever I go out people want to talk to me about tattoos. When I try to get help buying running shoes from a sales rep they just

want to talk tattoos and not fit or help me. My close friends get frustrated because if we go to a party it ends up with them standing around while I get hounded by people for information about tattoos, and half the time those people never actually come get them.

AA

Thornton notes that the conversion of subcultural capital to economic capital does not occur as easily as it may do between *cultural* capital and economic (Thornton, 1995:12). However, I would argue that subcultural capital within the tattoo community is more complex than Thornton's comparison suggests. IK's and AA's narratives illustrate the notable difference between the capital held by the profession as a whole – which can be held both inside and outside of the community – and the capital of the individual artists – usually granted by the 'insiders' of the community. It is the capital held by individual artists that ultimately leads to the production of economic capital. Tattoo artists gain economic capital by becoming well-known, respected artists in the community, and this capital is legitimised by influential individuals within the community such as bloggers, magazine editors and fellow artists who already hold status and power. Social media platforms such as Instagram have been integral in recent years in the promotion of artists' work (Force, 2022), and this too has an impact on capital – the number of followers and 'likes' on posts are all ways that an artist can accumulate more capital. Artists with less sub-cultural capital may continue to earn a living from tattooing, but this financial reward generally only increases if their sub-cultural capital also increases. More sub-cultural capital leads to a higher status in the community and likely more financial success. Artists who are influential in popularising new styles or techniques of tattooing become the sub-cultural authors of the community and gain respect for their role in defining and creating the industry as well as holding capital for their role as a tattooer.

Television and the Kat Von D Effect

Kat Von D is somewhat of an interesting example of how complex sub-cultural capital can be. Her reputation amongst the insiders and outsiders of the sub-culture has led to ambivalence towards her work and influence on tattoo culture, and although her popularity has waned somewhat in recent years, her influence was something addressed throughout the participant interviews and is important for me to address.

Kat Von D (KVD) first appeared on screen in the TLC television series, *Miami Ink* (Thompson, 2019). She then acquired her own series, *LA Ink*, in 2007. This showed KVD and her colleagues working in the LA studio *High Voltage Tattoo*, and as discussed in Chapter 2, was seen to bring tattoo culture to the masses in many respects. It was no surprise, therefore, when KVD came up in conversation during the interviews:

She's empowered women artists in the industry, I think. It's far more accessible to women now, and I can only assume that's partly down to her raising the profile of TALENTED women in the industry. Granted it's a slow process, but I do think attitudes are changing. The public's perception of women tattooists is rapidly gaining momentum, sadly I think the industry itself has some catching up to do.

EK

Often the publics' opinion and the industry opinion of her [KVD] differs: the public love her, the tradesmen not so much. I do think she has done good for the tattoo society in the publics' eyes in the way that a beautiful, popular woman can not only be covered in tattoos, but be one of the top artists within her field. I think it has given some female artists the opportunity to show they can do it too, or be brave enough to go into a studio and ask for that apprenticeship they've been dreaming of. On the other hand, whereas she was first known for her work, now she is known for being 'Kat von D'; herself. As it happens to many celebrities, she has been turned into a product, rather than producing herself.

YA

Here we can see the somewhat mixed opinions towards KVD and what she has or has not done for women in the industry. YA reflects discussions familiar to me both during the research process and outside of the research – often, public opinion of KVD differs greatly to the opinion of people inside of the industry. To outsiders, she is a familiar face, a successful artist who brought tattooing to the mainstream public; for the same reasons, she is somewhat disliked or not respected by artists inside of the industry. We cannot deny, however, the increased representation of women LA Ink and KVD has brought to the mainstream (Thompson, 2019). Interestingly EK, who we know to have come to tattooing from outside of the subculture, feels that KVD has been a positive influence for women artists. EK's opinion is perhaps informed by her initial status as an 'outsider' and, therefore, her standpoint differs from that of KB or HS, for example. YA does acknowledge that KVD may have had a positive influence for some women in the industry; however, like HS, she also criticises KVD for the marketing of herself as a product or a brand. This, of course, relates to the notion that tattooing is a business, and as such there is some marketing of the self required to become successful, as I will expand upon in the next chapter.

KVD's example shows that there is, it seems, a clash of capital amongst the tattooed community. Being well-known on the *inside* of the community is positive for artists. However, being well-known by people outside of the community is not so positive and alludes to the existence of 'authentic' and 'inauthentic' consumers. Insiders are regarded as authentic, whereas outsiders might be inauthentic and, therefore, the capital they award artists is not legitimate or warranted. To have value inside the community, as an artist, you must have the 'right' consumers. This clash of capital has been largely accelerated by the increased televisation of tattooing, which has been a significant and influential factor in the mainstreaming of tattooing, having a substantial effect upon the capital held by tattooers outside of the sub-culture. It has aided the dissemination of knowledge about the industry and tattooing as an artistic process, becoming the vehicle through which tattooing reaches a wider audience, leaving the industry open and visible to people outside of the tattooed community and reducing the 'secrecy' of the industry discussed previously, and favoured by KB. This further complicates the nuances surrounding the subcultural capital held inside and outside of the community, and the artists were keen to express their concerns surrounding the effect tattoo shows were having on the image of the industry.

> Nowadays it's 'cool' because it's on TV. People getting hands and necks tattooed before they have sleeves, with no regards to future careers. It's cool because you can get mega rich and famous. All your friends think you're amazing. It's easy money. I WISH!!! ... Don't get me wrong, they have done the tattoo industry a world of favours. For the first time, people see how good tattoos can be. Hannah Aitchinson on LA ink blew my mind. Her use of colour blending and her ability to draw the human form is just pure skill. People have started to want bigger pieces, and want something custom. It has encouraged people to look at tattooists work and realise the possibilities are endless. Also that different people specialise in different areas. It has made tattooing a very rich industry for certain people, and this is a good thing. Conventions have sprung up all over the place, people are generally much more interested in tattoo art.
>
> The downside... Everyone is a tattooist. It's received a 'cool' status and everyone wants to be Kat von D or Ami James. I guess I may be contradicting my last question answer, because that's what drew me in 10 years ago.
>
> KB

KB, having previously said that she liked the status and the 'celebrity' attention that being a tattooer might bring, here expresses her disappointment that tattooing is now considered 'cool' due to the wider television coverage it attracts. Although, as I have previously discussed, this suggests that capital earned from being on TV (and in turn the mainstreaming of tattooing) is, in the eyes of some artists, the 'wrong' kind of capital and possibly, therefore, not 'legitimate' or meaningful, it also illustrates the ambivalence felt towards the mainstream attention given to tattooing. This reflects what Breeze (2015) discusses in relation to roller derby and the mainstream, in that to be taken seriously when engaging in alternative or resistant practices, one may have to conform to hegemonic and dominant ideologies (2015:27). In the case of tattooing, these dominant ideologies might manifest as mainstream media representations of tattooing, for example. Conforming to mainstream media leads to complexities: although the media publicises tattooing, and, therefore, may increase the chances of the mainstream taking tattooing seriously as a profession, some media portrayals are far from positive, and, therefore, do not promote seriousness at all. On the one hand, television appears to have increased the amount of capital afforded to tattoo artists, but on the other hand, diluted this capital in many ways.

> A client's expectation now is probably informed my shows like Miami Ink etc.
>
> The amount of times I have been asked if I watch these shows is...almost every client.
>
> I have seen perhaps half an episode.
>
> Tattooing is a slog of a job.
>
> NT

> You have the disadvantage that everybody thinks they know all about it, but you also have the advantage that people have opened their minds to tattooing. But, it is a very double-edged sword. It has unfortunately bought a lot of "entitlement syndrome" in to it. Because they see it and think that's cool, with some people, that's the only thing they know about tattoo.. it got to a point where a lot of other artists wanted to get t-shirts printed saying, "yes I've f*cking seen LA Ink..."
>
> HS

Here HS illustrates the clash of capital. Increased coverage of tattoo in the mainstream means that the non-tattooed public 'think they know all about it', but at the same time, HS talks positively of people having their minds opened to tattooing as an artistic practice. Knowledge gained via the television shows is often used as capital currency within the community; both HS and NT, as illustrated above, have experienced 'outsiders' to the tattoo community using the shows to gain capital, attempting to use the shows as a familiar cultural reference or perhaps using culturally specific language to display knowledge of the sub-culture. This, therefore, is deemed an 'inauthentic' performance of identity, as the initial introduction and socialisation into the culture was via media representation of the culture's ideologies and not direct socialisation from members of the subculture (Dupont, 2014:571). If the media are presenting both 'inauthentic' and 'authentic' information about the subculture, the outsider does not have the ability or knowledge to decipher what is and what is not legitimate information, and this is ultimately what 'gives them away' as outsiders (Dupont, 2014:571).

Television was also criticised for the unrealistic image it portrayed of the industry and of tattooing as a practice.

TV makes it look so damn easy. Back pieces tattooed in 15 minutes. Sleeves drawn up in seconds. Every tattooist being utterly loaded with cash. Getting drunk all night and tattooing all day. Why wouldn't you want to be a tattoo artist?? I feel that this had bred a society of really bad tattooers, and really greedy business men. I know of people who run tattoo shops, that have no interest in tattoos. They get any old bedroom tattooist in and take half their money. That's fine I guess. It's just heart breaking when you know there are amazing artists short of work, and these awful tattooers are booked up.

KB

...her [Kat Von D] show presents tattooing in such an unrealistic light. Because of that show people think they can come in at 11: 00pm and get a full sleeve done. It's crazy! It happens all the time. I'll try to explain to someone that it takes ten hours sometimes just to DRAW a sleeve, let alone another twenty plus to tattoo it, and they just can't believe it... All these tattoo shows that are popping up are ridiculous. I don't follow them religiously, but I've scoped them out for obvious reasons.

AA

Both KB and AA refer to the unrealistic expectations that television shows perpetuate, suggesting perhaps the shows demeaned the skill involved in tattooing, which, in turn, diminished the hard work that goes into developing a career in the field. This has a detrimental effect on the respect held for artists outside of the industry, leading to a decrease in legitimacy. Artists want to be considered as hard-working professionals outside of the sub-culture, in the hope that this reduces the stigma attached to the industry, but many artists feel that television reality shows are presenting tattooing as a glamourous and 'easy' career. Because of this, there was ambivalence towards the effect television has upon the industry.

Of course, conflict also arises between the effect of television on the mainstreaming of the sub-culture, and the effect of television on the opportunity for financial gain and economic capital, as illustrated here by LC:

I feel totally disoriented about the way that subcultures in general are going. It seems like marketing and internet proliferation of images has really recontextualized every symbol or sign of subcultural membership. I like some elements of pop culture, and I benefit from tattooing being popular, but there is part of me that is forlorn to see subversive symbolism turn normal. I do love tattoos though, I think that tattoos really add character and beauty so I'm excited to see more and more people getting tattoos you can see. Conflicted I guess?

LC

As LC identifies, there is a conflict here, and an ambivalence towards the effects of mainstreaming on what was a sub-cultural activity. Although tattoo artists may criticise the mainstreaming of their sub-cultural practices, they are also benefiting from this popularisation: through being taken more seriously as a profession, and financially. This is an issue any subculture would face upon its aesthetics, signs and symbols being more widely accepted in the mainstream, and it is something that the artists in the tattooing industry must negotiate. This is demonstrated through an ambivalence towards the mainstreaming of tattoo culture, and continuous conflicts and contradictions are seen throughout many of the interviews.

The 'Other' Artist

In Chapter 2, I highlighted the significance of 'the other' in the subcultural narratives. Building upon discussions by Lane (2021), Thompson (2015), and Dann (2021), the creation of 'the other' was also a recurring dialogue within my own research. Placing themselves in comparison to other artists seemed important to the women and this was key to the narratives; it was very much part of the interviewees' identity work and performances of the self which, in turn, created a platform for them to reinforce their professional standing (Gimlin, 2010:74).

> I think being a tattooist is so 'cool' at the minute, and there are so many awful tattooers in the UK at the minute.
>
> KB

> I feel that if tattooing wasn't such an accessible, cool thing, the weak would be weeded out and we would be left with a client base of serious tattoo collectors, and quality work across the board.
>
> KB

> A friend of mine in her 50's who tattoos, said she was working a convention a while ago and being spoken to like an idiot by some 20-year-old hipster kid, he's only been tattooing 5 minutes, did one style of tattoo and yet called himself an old-school tattooist. We said, no, an old-school tattooist did whatever came in the door, you'd be there from 10am to 8pm at night, doing every style that was thrown at you, you had to up for every style, not this neo-traditional thing.
>
> HS

There was always an 'other' to resist against, somebody 'not' to be, with many of the participants criticising artists for their lack of skill, lack of authenticity or illegitimacy. Distancing the self from 'bad' artists not only indicates a devotion and a passion for 'good' tattoos, but it also serves as a tool for constructing the self as a 'good' artist. 'Bad' artists are not named specifically, but similarly to the women discussing 'other' careers at the beginning of this chapter, they are used as symbolic others by which the interviewees can then construct their own identity around, or in direct comparison to. The artists also use 'othering' to discursively position themselves within the industry hierarchy (Demello, 2000:6) and legitimise their own space within the field – creating dichotomies to produce and display their own 'authentic' subcultural identities (Becker, 1966, cited in Dupont, 2014):

> There are 2 studios in our town, one is *ahem* questionable, and the other has been established for 3 years, but I've done a lot of cover up of his work.
>
> EK

Here we see EK not only claiming that another tattooist in her town was 'questionable', but telling us that she has covered up his work – demonstrating clearly that EK is placing her own work as *better* than his. HS, who had been tattooing for the longest out of all of my interviewees, criticised the younger generation of tattoo artists and used her age and years of tattooing experience as proof of authenticity and capital to place herself above 'them' within the hierarchy, even though she herself had experienced discrimination as a younger tattoo artist:

> My age (I was 21) often worked more against me [than gender], which of course I understand completely now!!
>
> HS

Some of the artists also described being 'othered' by their fellow artists, although didn't recognise that this is what they had been doing themselves.

> I can feel very judged by other tattooed people- just like in any subculture, some of them are snobbish about it or take it to the extreme - if you don't have what's 'cool' right now, then they will look down on you. This is definitely noticeable when tattooists meet 'scratchers' (the derogatory term tattooists have for artists like me who taught themselves). Though not always - again, it just comes down to if the person is respectful and comfortable with themselves.
>
> IK

> From experience, the customers don't care [that I am a woman] once they've seen what I can do... It's most certainly other artists that create the feeling of being ostracized.
>
> EK

Both IK and EK suggest that it is fellow artists who impose and reinforce the hierarchy or at least the feeling of a hierarchical structure. The hierarchy is imposed by and amongst the artists themselves. The term 'scratcher' used here by IK is, as discussed in Chapter 2, a common term within tattooing circles, and is used to describe any artist who is either self-taught (as opposed to learning through an apprenticeship) or who does not fulfil the artistic skills and expectations of whomever is doing the describing. It is usually used by tattoo artists or by established, long-term members of the tattoo community with derogatory intent. It is an example of what Thornton has termed 'embodied subcultural capital' – being 'in the know' – and might be displayed through using language specific to the subculture or community, for example (Thornton, 1995:11). Embodied subcultural capital could also be displayed by using other language specific to the subculture, and would only be accessible and intelligible to people who had some involvement with the community – for instance, KB, who affiliated with the community for a long time before she began tattooing, would have the ability to 'talk the talk' and, therefore, openly display her embodied subcultural capital. This again can be used to distinguish the 'insiders' and the 'outsiders' of the community; mirroring the inauthentic consumers, scratchers are considered inauthentic producers, and this reproduces hierarchies amongst artists.

Voicing their commitment to the industry was another way in which artists placed themselves on the cultural hierarchy. Status and authenticity is claimed by displaying very high levels of commitment to the subculture, in comparison to other 'less committed' members of the subculture (Dupont, 2014:561). The artists also used the retelling of other people's experiences rather than their own, when giving examples of how the industry treats them – by doing this, the interviewees were reasserting the discourses and narratives that they want to be heard (Gimlin, 2010:60–1). This is especially evident when some of the women talk about male artists and the masculinities evident in the industry – not all of the women have personal experience of dominant masculinities, but most offer examples, either of their own experiences or of others'. Men artists were certainly, for some women, seen as somebody to compare themselves to, with some of the participants creating a gendered 'other'. This serves to emphasise the existence of a sub-cultural dominant masculinity – whether experienced personally or not. This, as discussed in Chapter 2, refers to Thornton's (1995) 'imagined other' and is not necessarily how the subculture is organised but is more to do with how members of the community imagine or see their social world, measure their cultural worth and claim their subcultural capital in comparison to fellow members of the group (Thornton, 1995:96).

Gendered Authenticity

Throughout the interviews the women described what appeared to be a masculinised culture within the industry. The narratives show recurring themes surrounding the dominance of masculinity within the field of tattooing and what I would identify as gendered norms and understanding of authenticity of knowledge and status. Subcultural capital is often biased towards masculinity, which can, in some circumstances, leave femininity holding a marginal status, mirroring that of wider cultural situations (Brill, 2007:112). Issues of legitimisation and authenticity are key in the accumulation and the displaying of subcultural capital, and in the case of my research it appeared that authenticity in the field of tattooing was heavily gendered.

> In my experience, the public are FAR more open to women tattooists and are almost excited by the prospect of seeing what women can do in a predominantly male industry. Other artists though are a whole other ball game. It's a period of proving oneself before you're accepted as capable as a man.
>
> EK

> Women in this industry constantly have to fight for the respect that is thrown, all too often undeservedly, at men... I actually can't recall an instance where a client made a remark about the sex of the men I work with and its effect on their tattooing.
>
> AA

Although EK's and AA's quotes are slightly contradictory in that AA has experienced client (as well as men artists) discrimination against women artists, both narratives suggest that the masculine culture of the industry legitimises men's knowledge over women's and places men as the legitimate, authorised holders of knowledge and power. It also has a significant effect upon how women artists negotiate their femininity, and this was an important theme to come out of the interviews. The women spoke about having to 'prove themselves' as capable tattooers and how, at times, they struggled to be 'taken seriously'. I would argue that this is a direct result of a hegemonic masculinity in the industry, and it is a significant part of being a woman artist in a male-dominated and masculinised field. Interestingly, the term 'rock star' was frequently used to describe men in the industry.

> I have come across some men who think they're something akin to young rock gods.
>
> There's a lot of hero worship that goes on.
>
> NT

> I have worked along one or two 'Rock Star' tattooists, but that doesn't really bother me as an artist.
>
> YA

> It was a bit of a rock star job. I've heard so many stories about [tattoo artist] (I mentioned I apprenticed in his old shop) having a studio full

of walk in customers and turning them all away because he wanted to play his guitar all day. People still came back.

KB

Here we see women describe a very specific form of masculinity which they perceive to be dominant in the tattoo sub-culture. This 'rock star' version of masculinity seems to draw on the stereotype of a creative or artistic man with an inflated ego, demanding and receiving attention and adulation. There has been a connection between western tattooing and rock music for a long time – which might explain the literal association of men artists with the term 'rock god'. However, I would argue that the association goes further than that. It also alludes to a rock star 'attitude', perhaps being edgy, dangerous and assertive whilst demanding sexualised attention from customers/fans, with their sub-cultural capital enabling a sense of entitlement to this attention. This is a good example of how the dominant sub-cultural norms of masculinity are reproduced within the sub-culture and are specific to the sub-culture itself. The women were also perhaps using the term 'rock star' to devalue the capital afforded to men artists, in an attempt to mock this hegemonic form of masculinity and gain distinction themselves (Vroomen, 2002:126), evidencing perhaps another form of negotiating gendered power imbalances.

The recurrent and performative role of this 'rock star' masculinity suggests a certain type of hegemonic masculinity, one which is specific to tattoo culture. Hegemonic masculinity legitimises men's dominant position in any given culture and society, at the same time as justifying the subordination of women and 'policing marginalised expressions of gendered manhood' (Wilz, 2019:49). The hegemonic masculinity experienced within tattoo culture may differ from wider societal hegemonic masculinities, but will, like any hegemonic version of masculinity, be created and enforced through the production and reproduction of norms – whether these norms are sub-cultural or societal. Hegemonic masculinity does not represent a certain *type of man*, but a way in which men position themselves through discursive practices – men can adopt the symbolic indicators of the hegemonic masculinity if needed or wanted but at the same time, can distance themselves from it also (Connell and Messerschmidt, 2005:842). Many of the men who enact the hegemonic masculinity of the tattoo sub-culture will not fit with the norms of masculinity *outside* of the sub-culture. And so, when I discuss a hegemonic masculinity, I mean a sub-culturally specific hegemony, and the dominant norms of masculinity that the sub-culture reproduces.

In comparison to the assumed 'rock star' status of the men artists, women artists are often placed in a position of 'props' and assistants to the men in the studios.

You get the odd, older gentleman client, that still thinks women don't belong in a tattoo shop and automatically assumes you are the receptionist.

KB

> It is frustrating when people assume I am the assistant, but their ignorance is nothing to me, it just pushes me to prove myself more. I know I am capable, let me show it!
>
> YA

Ignored, miscategorised or disrespected, the women artists are left having to prove themselves as legitimate producers of their own standing, further demonstrating the masculine culture of the industry. Although YA describes this as frustrating, she also argues that the presumption that she is an assistant pushes her to prove herself. YA expresses this as something positive, but it also illustrates the weight of the continuous negotiation and labour that many women artists have to deploy in order to be taken seriously as artists in the sub-culture. To be taken seriously in a male-dominated and masculine culture, there is a certain degree of conforming to the masculine ideal required to succeed (Breeze, 2015; LeBlanc, 1999).

> I have worked alongside an amazing female tattoo artist, she advised me on how to hold myself in front of male artists. For instance, not having all of my equipment pink, might allow me to be taken more seriously...celebrating being a 'girlie' girl with pink tattoo machines and pigtails, might lead to some of the more 'old school' artists not taking that woman seriously as an artist. I would say that definitely some people see pink equipment as too feminine. First impressions count, not even tattooing escapes this. I think women no matter what profession, are under scrutiny a little more than our male counterparts, so we may just have to work a little harder to prove our worth. We have a certain image to hold, in every walk of life. I guess it is about 'fitting in with the boys', or perhaps just playing down on our femininity. Be recognised as an artist before being noticed for being a woman, and that may just get us the respect we deserve. This industry has been predominantly male for years, female artists just need to prove that they have every right to be there too.
>
> YA

Femininity, or exaggerated and overt femininity – what YA describes here as using pink equipment or being a 'girlie girl' (something I take to mean adhering in an explicit and even exaggerated way to dominant norms of what it means to be feminine) – seems to imply a 'lack' in the field: lack of skills and knowledge, and a lack of worth and seriousness. YA was 'taught' how to manage herself in front of men artists; this suggests that women are not taken seriously and must actively, consciously and strategically manage their femininity in order to gain respect. Femininity, or at least 'too much femininity', is seen as something to be toned down, to be able to 'fit in with the boys' and succeed. YA even says that women need to be seen as artists first, women second, to be taken seriously; this highlights the problematic relationship the masculine industry has with women trying to succeed, suggesting a degree of invisibility is required until the women have proved that they are worthy of the respect afforded to men artists.

I discussed above how the industry has, to some degree, had to conform to mainstream norms and ideologies to be taken seriously as a profession and an industry. Here we see that women, in order to be taken seriously as capable tattoo artists, not only have to conform to *mainstream* norms, but also to internal industry and sub-cultural norms and ideologies. In Chapter 2, I discussed Breeze's use of the 'feminine apologetic' and the feminisation of 'masculine' activities. Here we see that the feminisation of tattoo equipment is seen, by women, as something to avoid and so rather than over-playing feminine aesthetics to apologise for being a woman in a supposedly man's role, women tattoo artists are downplaying feminine aesthetics in order to be taken seriously. This, it seems, is a different type of feminine apologetic – rather than over-playing femininity as a way of reassuring women are no threat to the masculine order, women tattooists downplay their femininity in an attempt to 'fit in' with the men. Although not all the women had personal experience of this dominant masculinity, most had anecdotal narratives shared by clients, which suggests the hegemonic gender order is not reserved for the industry but is present throughout the sub-culture.

It is important to note at this point, however, that just as hegemonic masculinities between different cultures (such as the tattoo sub-culture and the mainstream, for example) are multiple and complex, hegemonic masculinities *within* cultures are also complex. Arguing for the existence of a hegemonic masculinity does not mean arguing that 'masculinity' is a fixed entity or indeed that the dominant masculinities are the embodied reality of all men and the male artists in the industry. Suggesting that there is a hegemonic masculinity evident within the tattoo industry does not mean to say that all male artists are complicit in this. The hegemonic masculinity of the industry does not only affect women – studios are often very masculine spaces, whether they intend to be or not. Just as men who conform to the sub-cultural norms of masculinity might not fit with wider societal ideals of masculinity, not all men within the sub-culture adhere to the dominant sub-cultural norms of masculinity. This can be intimidating for anybody who does not 'fit' into this category of masculinity and can often leave some men feeling like they are expected to conform to a narrow set of masculine ideals. This was identified by some of the women I interviewed, who could see that some men clients are affected by the hegemonic masculinity and found women artists easier to work with.

> A friendly face is often welcomed. I have been told in the past by men that they felt uncomfortable walking into male ran studios, whereas with me they feel at ease. . . I do believe the accessibility of female tattooists now has led to the more nervous of society to be able to get tattooed.
>
>   YA

What this quote does not acknowledge is that it is not only men clients who might experience the effects of a hegemonic masculinity, but men artists also, who may feel a pressure to conform to the culture's dominant norms of masculinity. When getting tattooed, clients are often apprehensive for various reasons: worried about the level of physical pain, how the body will respond to the pain or the awkwardness of being in intimate proximity with a stranger, for example. Here YA talks about a 'friendly face' and how female tattooists may help the more nervous of clients to get tattooed. By adopting traditionally male roles, women are changing the industry and, in turn, the sub-culture – if what YA suggests here is true, more people who do not fit the mould of the hegemonic masculinity of the community are now able to get tattooed; this masculinity could in time become diluted and the community and industry might feel less of a male dominated space; this is something I explore in more depth in the next chapter. Additional to this, I must note that although the participants spoke about the masculine nature of the industry, some of the women also wanted to express their positive experiences of working with men artists. Both NT and HS discussed men artists in a positive light, suggesting that women who might have had experiences of the masculine culture as a whole were keen to express more positive experiences they had had with individual men artists.

> Some of my biggest mentors have been male. I wouldn't want to take away from their input. I have worked with a lot of male artists who not at any stage have treated me any less because I am a woman. The guys you think are more old fashioned, would never talk down to me because I was a woman.
>
> HS

> And from my experience when women artists are talked about by male artists it is with total equality based on their skill.
>
> NT

Both HS and NT's personal experiences illustrate that, as I have discussed above, suggesting that the tattoo sub-culture is a masculinised space, which constructs norms of a hegemonic masculinity, does not mean that *all* men artists conform to this set of norms. However, HS, who here wanted to express her positive experiences with most of the male artists she has worked with, also told me about the difficulties she experienced when she had her daughter.

> Sadly in this industry (even though you would hope it would be better being an 'alternative' type of industry) male run studios are not always understanding of child care issues for women. This is something that I find is generally not a problem for men! I have been very disappointed by my experiences in this field. Thankfully where I work now has been much better about it and more understanding but my eyes have been fully opened by my experiences since having a child.

> Maybe if one day, I do have my own place it will all be run around
> childcare hours for female artists!
>
> HS

We should not presume, therefore, that subcultures do not come with the same issues as more mainstream workplaces. HS describes an expectation that because she is working in an alternative industry, it would be different from mainstream employment and yet, she was disappointed to find in many ways, it was the same. Working in an alternative career still means having to perform this career within the constraints of more mainstream norms and values; it does not avoid them completely. What HS offers here is evidence that the tattoo industry is, in part, no different from any other mainstream employment in that it, along with many other industries, has an issue in dealing with the practicalities of working parents – something that HS identifies as being predominantly an issue for women workers rather than their men colleagues.

'One of the Boys'?

I would argue that it is not only men who can adopt the hegemonic masculinity, and my interviews show this. We cannot argue that hegemonic masculinity is adopted through discursive practices and is not inherent in all men, without acknowledging that women can, therefore, adopt these discursive practices too. In contrast to the women who criticised the masculinity within the industry, there were artists who embraced this specific form of masculinity, and worked with it rather than actively resisted it. The way in which the women had come to negotiate the masculinities differed and depended upon their subcultural habitus, socialisation and route into tattooing. Whatever their methods of negotiation, the women were all very aware that this negotiation was taking place and voiced this through their narratives.

> I've always been a bit of a tomboy so I knew that I had to pick a
> job in an atmosphere I would be comfortable in, i.e. a male
> dominated one [...] I have no problem working alongside men. I
> usually find their behaviour amusing! But as I have mentioned
> earlier, I've always been a bit of a tomboy, so I am used to being
> around men. A lot of women aren't like this.
>
> YA

> I have been one of the boys since my teens [...] In a tattoo shop (as
> well as a band) when you are the only female, you are subjected to
> a lot of 'man banter'. I always join in.
>
> KB

Both KB and YA recognise the dominant masculinity in the industry and refer to their previous experience of male-dominated subcultures. KB and YA both have access to, and the ability to appropriate typical masculine traits, which they express here as being an important part of their identity. Research on gender and gender negotiation in subcultures has explored the notion of the 'tomboy' and has argued that rather than disrupting the gender order of any male-dominated field, it serves to reinforce and reproduce the male vs female power relations (Scraton et al., 1999:105). Backstrom, in their research on gender and skateboarding, notes that in the skateboarding subculture, displaying tomboy femininities is met with an accepted presence within the hegemonic gender order (Backstrom, 40:2013). This suggests that identifying as a tomboy or 'one of the boys', rather than offering any kind of alternative femininity, is, in fact, colluding with the male dominance and, therefore, perpetuating the gendered hegemony within the field. To claim that KB and YA are 'colluding' with male dominance is, I think, somewhat disparaging and over simplistic. Their relationship with and negotiation of the masculinities and femininities of the field are far more nuanced than this argument would recognise. In her research on gender and rock music, Schippers (2002) introduces the concept of gender manoeuvring – a concept that can help us to understand the dynamics and nuances of what KB and YA express here. Schippers explores strategies employed to transform sexist cultures into non-sexist ones and explains gender manoeuvring as being *cultural* and *interactive*. *Cultural* refers to the manipulation of relationships between masculinity and femininity as culturally embedded beliefs, and *interactive* refers to the manipulation of these relationships in moments of interaction (Schippers, 2002). The concept of gender manoeuvring allows us to explore the relationships between genders as actively negotiated within face-to-face interactions (Schippers, 2002). The intention of gender manoeuvring is to transform the gender relations and organisations of everyday life with 'our bodies, our activities, our interactions, and in the broader distribution of resources and power' (Schippers, 2002:189). It is not simply a case of KB and YA colluding and, therefore, reinforcing the gender order; I do believe that their access to masculine habitus was influential in their ability to gain space within the field (which I will expand upon below). However, later in their interviews, both women spoke about knowingly using their femininity for the benefit of not only themselves, but also other women in the tattoo community. Therefore, this active negotiation between 'fitting in' with the male culture of the field but positively utilising their femininity within this male space could be seen as gender manoeuvring.

Previously I have argued that subcultural capital is an influential factor in women artists gaining space within the field of tattooing, but we also need to consider the effect of a masculine habitus and how this may impact gaining entry to the industry. For example, although KB possessed capital from her affiliation with the tattoo community before her career as a tattooist, both KB and YA have previously associated with other male-dominated subcultures and, therefore, possess embodied masculine capital. They know how to present themselves in a male-dominated environment. Neither KB nor YA criticise the masculine culture of the industry, and we could argue that this is because they have been socialised into it. We could, therefore, also argue that KB and YA have both been welcomed into the industry so readily because of their willingness to accept the hegemonic masculinity. Anyone trained through an apprenticeship is nurtured and socialised in what is predominantly a masculine space. The hegemonic masculinity is 'the norm' and becomes embodied. Those artists who have affiliated with the community before becoming a tattooer have spent even longer being socialised into the dominant masculine culture and, therefore, may appropriate certain aspects of the hegemonic masculinity (Connell and Messerschmidt, 2005:847). The women who can recognise this male dominance, but rather than resist it, work with it, are perhaps more likely to be 'accepted' into it. Finley, in her research on women's roller derby recognises that in subcultures, women, as with any subordinate group, are sometimes driven to using the resources available to them to 'survive', and therefore, Finley suggests it is likely that women negotiate between multiple femininities in differing contexts (2010:362–3). Finley also notes that some of the multiple femininities performed, may be of benefit to other women within the patriarchal system, and some may not (Finley, 2010:362–3). This then may lead to some women being seen as conforming to dominant norms of femininity to succeed – as Reddington (2003) notes in her work on punk subculture, that to be successful in a male-dominated sphere, women must package themselves as objects 'amenable to men' (2004:249). In the same way that Tseelon (1995) identified a 'feminine masquerade', we could argue that an appropriation of masculine capital could be a *masculine masquerade* – women embodying and performing aspects of hegemonic masculinity in an attempt to forge relationships in certain situational contexts. Women can adopt the traits of hegemonic masculinity in order to access masculine cultural capital. Once they have gained a space in the industry by appropriating masculinised traits or at least 'fitting in' with the culture in which these traits are performed, they are able to engage in behaviours associated more with dominant versions of femininity, to benefit themselves and their clients; I will discuss this further in the next chapter.

Conclusion

By examining the artists' route from consumer to producer, this chapter introduces and highlights some of the key themes to have emerged from the research. Many of the women chose to pursue a career in tattooing as an alternative to mainstream employment. After already engaging with alternative subcultures, life as a tattoo artist offered potential for them to 'be themselves' in the workplace, extending their alternative lifestyle from one associated with youth culture to one of work and adulthood. Some of the artists discussed 'other' forms of employment, and described how mainstream employment was restrictive and relied on the compromising of the self and identities. The field is perceived, and in some cases, voiced and presented as a space of freedom. However, as discussions progressed, contradictions emerged.

What this chapter identifies is that this space of freedom comes with many restrictions and boundaries. Not all the artists had found it easy to break into the industry, and what emerged was a prominent hegemonic masculine culture, perpetuated by male gatekeepers, creating barriers for women striving to make the transition from tattoo client or enthusiast to tattoo artist. The chapter not only illustrates the capital afforded to male artists, and what constitutes authorised and legitimised knowledge, but it also highlights the masculinities at play within the field.

The hegemonic masculinity of the culture also led to a gendered authenticity, whereby men's knowledge was considered more authentic and legitimate than women's. This left many of the women feeling as though they had to work harder to be taken seriously in the field – by both fellow artists and consumers. The industry, it appeared, is built upon hierarchies – both gendered and sub-cultural and revolves around fluid and unstable power imbalances that require careful and complex reflexivity and manoeuvring.

Capital was a central theme to emerge from this chapter, with complex and nuanced discussions illustrating the paradoxes and ambivalence attached to capital within tattoo culture. Sub-cultural capital had facilitated some of the women's transition from consumer to producer, although the same women still described difficulties in gaining space in the field. This sub-cultural capital was coupled with socialisation into tattoo culture, which implied that some women could access, utilise and appropriate a masculine habitus to 'fit in' to the hegemonic masculine norms of the field and, therefore, were sometimes more likely to be accepted by their men colleagues. Although this might, by some, be considered as colluding with the masculine hegemony, it also illustrates the fluidity and plurality of the masculinities and femininities, and highlights the ability to utilise, appropriate and combine different gendered behaviours, which is something I explore further in subsequent chapters.

This chapter also identified contradictions and ambivalence in discussions around sub-cultural capital. Participants spoke about the popularisation of tattooing in the mainstream, and how their capital and status as artists, although being vital to success and, therefore, welcomed within the industry, capital held outside of the sub-culture, led to feelings of ambivalence. Tattooists benefit financially from the increase in interest in tattooing, but felt ambivalence towards tattooing becoming more popular in the mainstream. Television was seen to be a key influence in the mainstreaming of the tattoo, but artists who had appeared on TV or had been involved in TV shows were seen as having 'sold out'. There was discussion around consumers and the capital they grant artists. Authentic consumers, who were seen as committed to the subculture, were respected and appreciated. Inauthentic consumers, however, (for example, individuals who had gained their tattoo knowledge through TV and mainstream media) were less respected and their opinions not valued.

This chapter identifies the clashes of capital within the subculture and the industry, the conflict between insiders and outsiders, and the demonstration of authentic and non-authentic consumers. It also reveals a significant hegemonic masculinity dominating the culture, and because of this, subcultural authenticity is invisibly gendered. Women as both tattooed people and tattoo artists strive to distance themselves from both mainstream ideals of femininity, and the 'other' artists (what they deem 'bad' artists, for example). However, women artists are at the same time in a position of being the other, with regards to being a woman in the industry. How then, does this affect the ways in which women negotiate their femininity within the field? And in what ways do women artists make femininity work for them?

Chapter 4

Making 'Woman' Work

So far, we have seen femininity as something to be downplayed or managed; this chapter will seek to explore how femininity and femaleness are actively employed and navigated within the field, and to ask what effect this might have upon the industry – thus complicating the analysis of negotiations of femininity, by introducing to the discussion the idea that femininity is also something to be positively utilised by tattoo artists. It was clear from the interviews that using aspects of their femininity was important to the artists and a prominent part of their lives as tattooers. I will focus upon women's experiences in the tattooing workplace and the relationship between the artist and the client, with a focus on gendered capital. This is a complex relationship and in continuing the exploration of this, the chapter will consider tattooing as body work and the emotional and aesthetic labour involved in the practice of tattooing. In the exploration of body work, I will utilise the work of Carol Wolkowitz who has previously argued that research on emotional labour has neglected the specific issue of workers' interactions with the bodies of clients, patients and customers where the work involves intimate bodily contact (Wolkowitz, 2006:146). Inspired by Wolkowitz, I argue that we must acknowledge the link between body work and emotional labour in tattooing. Discussions surrounding aesthetic labour will offer insights into how women artists manage the image of the profession outside of the tattooing community, and the labour employed to manage and negotiate these societal perceptions.

Capitalising the Female

The notion of gendered capital was born from an extension of Bourdieu's concept of cultural capital (see Lovell, 2000; McCall, 1992; Skeggs, 1997) and suggests that women can use gender as a form of capital or resource, developing femaleness and femininity as forms of embodied cultural capital which place the subject in a more active, powerful role in the construction of identity and agency (Ross-Smith and Huppatz, 2010:549). Research on gendered capital in the workplace includes the caring profession (Huppatz, 2009) and management (Ross-Smith and Huppatz, 2010), and similarities with the field of tattooing can be seen in relation to how gendered capital is utilised and valued.

Tattooing and the Gender Turn, 59–81
Copyright © 2023 Emma Beckett
Published under exclusive licence by Emerald Publishing Limited
doi:10.1108/978-1-80262-301-720231004

Huppatz' (2009) research on women in the caring industry introduces the notion of both *feminine* and *female* capital, and it is this that is so significant to my own work. It is important to note that the concepts of femininity and feminine capital are not seen as attributes reserved for women only, much like the discussion in the previous chapter surrounding masculinity not being the reserve of men or men artists. One must not fall into the essentialist trap of associating typically feminine traits with that of being a woman. Female capital is the gender advantage that is derived from being perceived as *female*, but not necessarily *feminine*. Feminine capital is the gender advantage that is derived from displaying traits associated with femininity (Huppatz, 2009:50) which, of course, are not exclusive to women. So how is this capital played out within the field of tattooing?

The existence of gender capital was broadly expressed throughout the artists' narratives in two ways. Firstly, many of the participants were eager for me to know that women clients often favoured women tattoo artists and sought them specifically because of their gender, thus indicating the existence of a form of female capital. Secondly, the artists were equally as keen to tell me about how they utilised their femininity to benefit their clients, which, in turn, increases their ability to gain economic capital. Female and feminine capital, although not named as such in the interviews, are a significant part of the women's narratives, shaping how they viewed themselves within the community and further constructed their role within the field. It was apparent that this was important to many of the women I interviewed and something which they took very seriously in their role as tattooer.

> [...] most of my customers are female, and so it [being a woman] attracts them as a customer base.
>
> KB

> I know a lot of women seek me out specifically for tattoos as they find it difficult to find a tattooist they trust. Many, many clients are referred to me after they have had bad experiences at professional parlours - most women tell stories of being bullied, scoffed at or just simply ignored. I hear these tales over and over, and certainly, when I got the one studio tatt that I have, from a man, that is how I was treated as well. I certainly don't treat my clients this way- but then again, I don't treat anyone that way.
>
> IK

> A high proportion of my customers are female, and I know a lot of them feel more comfortable with me, as a woman, than if they were to hire a male artist. Walking into a tattoo studio, and putting yourself under the needle can be quite a daunting

experience, so if I can help ease this uncomfort [sic], simply by
being female and friendly then all the better.

YA

We can see here that female capital in the field of tattooing is a valuable
resource, and the narratives suggest that the women are aware of this. In the
previous chapter, I argued that the women's sub-cultural habitus influenced how
they dealt with, or viewed the masculinity of the industry; here we see that the
sub-cultural background of the artist has little or no effect upon their engagement
with feminine and female capital – the women accumulate and utilise gendered
capital regardless of their background or access to sub-cultural capital. IK, for
example, talked extensively throughout her interview about her gendered capital
(although she did not use this specific term) and yet she also expresses her dislike
of the masculine nature of the industry, and lacks the sub-cultural capital that
perhaps KB or YA both hold. The women talk about their female capital as
something unique to them as women artists, offering something that men cannot
access – alluding to a sense of pride throughout the narratives. Although being a
woman, for some, hinders opportunity and the ability to transition from consumer to producer within the industry, the narratives in my research show that
once a woman artist has gained a space in the field, being a woman holds capital
which has the potential to be converted into economic capital. There is an
interesting paradox between the women being aware that their gender affected
their entry into the industry, and them being aware that their gender can be used
in a positive way to affect their position and income once in the field. The very
reason women find it so difficult to break into the industry has the potential to
become the reason they succeed. Once women have overcome the industry
gatekeepers and secured space in the field, artists are able to develop their skills
and role within the industry and what once counted against them can become
their distinctive 'selling point'.

Tattooing has not been a typically feminised occupation and has been seen
traditionally as a working-class, masculine trade and so the negotiation of feminine and female capital differs to that of, for example, the caring profession.
Ross-Smith and Huppatz' (2010) research on women in management explores the
experiences of women who have gained positions in an inherently masculine field
and subsequently use their gendered capital to further establish their place in the
field; their research shows similarities to my own work.

The women who took part in our study have successfully entered
this field and this research therefore provides the opportunity to
examine whether female and feminine dispositions may operate as
capital in a field that has generally privileged masculine
embodiment.

(Ross-Smith and Huppatz, 2010:548)

The tattoo industry as a field is predominantly masculine, with men artists
taking a position of dominance and power, which gives them the ability to 'shape

the field of play' (Ross-Smith and Huppatz, 2010:548). Clients, as suggested by IK's quote above, may align feminine qualities such as caring and listening with being female, and presume that a woman artist, therefore, will not display the stereotypically masculinised traits IK speaks of.

Clients choosing women artists has the potential to complicate and disrupt the hegemonic gender order. It was evident from the narratives that many women clients seek women artists to avoid the overly and narrowly masculine norms of the industry. YA too identifies that simply by being a woman, she may be able to alleviate some of the discomfort felt by women clients. Many of the artists I interviewed realised the potential for gendered capital to disrupt the dynamics of the overly masculine, male-dominated industry.

> I think the macho tattoo culture will shift – so many women are getting in to tattooing, and a lot of shops are opening that are all women, or directly aimed at women. I think it's a great thing. Anything that allows women to feel safer, supported and appreciated is fully endorsed by me.
>
> IK

Here IK makes a direct link between the rise of women getting tattooed and the shift in the masculine culture of the community. She does not specifically link women seeking women artists; however, she does identify that studios are becoming more women-friendly. Although it has been argued by some scholars (Skeggs, 1997) that using feminine capital will not overturn power relations completely, perhaps in the context of the tattoo industry women do increase the potential to overturn the power imbalances of the field using both female and feminine gendered capital.

Capitalising the Feminine

Feminine capital differs from female capital in that it relies on the traits associated with 'being feminine' and, therefore, is not reserved for women, but can be utilised by anyone willing and able to perform femininity. The women interviewed expressed their feminine capital through narratives of typically caring behaviour. Like their female capital, it was something important to their identities as tattooers and they seemed to take pride in caring for and providing a positive experience for their clients. Skeggs (1997) argues that a feminine habitus is something performed, something that women 'do' rather than what they are. This is particularly relevant to those artists who describe using their femininity to make clients feel comfortable and cared for, but yet do not identify as 'feminine' in their everyday identities, such as KB and YA, who identify as 'one of the boys'. YA specifically describes performing this femininity for the benefit of her clients, and ultimately, the benefit of her reputation as an artist. Skeggs has also suggested that women do not get the praise that men might get for displaying femininity because it is presumed to be a natural disposition for women to display. But is this different for tattooed women?

> [...] because it is such a male dominated industry, it is presumed you must be 'tough' or 'hard' to exist within it.
>
> IK

Here IK suggests that there are assumptions made around women's identities and personalities due to the nature of the field – tattooed women are not only subverting society's ideals of what it is to *look* feminine, but if women are actively engaging in the tattooing industry, they are presumed to be lacking in typically 'feminine' traits such as caring or listening and, therefore, what it is to *be* feminine. Perhaps therefore, performing femininity *does* get rewarded because these are traits not expected of women who defy mainstream norms of femininity. Research by Vail (1999) on tattoo collectors reveals the importance clients put upon the experience of becoming tattooed. The interviews showed participants valued the quality of the tattooing experience, and saw it as holding more meaning, than the technical qualities of the tattoo itself (Vail, 1999:266) – illustrating that clients do benefit from, and appreciate, the emotional labour employed by the participants in my own research.

Although *female* capital is inaccessible to men artists, men artists do have the opportunity to appropriate aspects of *feminine* capital and this, in turn, has the potential to disrupt and subvert the culture of unequal gendered power relations so prevalent within the industry. It also holds potential for men seeking to distance themselves from the kind of masculinity that might be off putting to their clients. Some of the participants did begin to discuss their thoughts on men's utilisation of these qualities in the interviews, although their views differed and sometimes contradicted themselves.

> I do believe female tattooists can be more approachable, and offer a more comfortable service [...] Also, during the tattoo, I know that I am a lot more gentle than some other (particularly male) artists. I don't like to put my client through any more pain than is necessary. Now, I don't know for certain if it's because I am a girl that makes me like this as an artist, I would guess it may have something to do with the mothering instinct!
>
> YA

> It should be the quality of work that makes someone popular, that and the experience you as an artist give your client. This can be done by either gender of tattooer.
>
> YA

> In the actual [tattooing] interaction, there is so much care and attending to your client's comfort and body. I don't know if male socialized tattooers feel the same way, but I imagine they might.
>
> LC

> I think a lot of clients seeking out women tattoo artists have had negative experiences not being listened to, and can count on women tattoo artists to be more likely to listen and attend to their needs just due to the shape of female socialization.
>
> LC

Both YA and LC recognise that women clients may seek out women artists due to presumptions around typically feminine traits, and both question male artists' abilities to utilise these same traits. It is interesting that both YA and LC contradict themselves at different points in the interviews, but, like Holland and Harpin (2015), I do not see this as a problem or invalid data; instead, it shows how complex and contradictory the negotiation of gender in tattooing is (2015: 296). Putting gendered traits into practice and performing gendered norms is seemingly so complex, and YA and LC's contradictions further prove this. YA, although having previously identified as 'one of the boys', offers the 'mothering instinct' as an explanation for her caring and gentle nature when tattooing, suggesting she puts this down to an innate 'feminine' quality in women. Although identifying with more masculine identities, overall, YA intimated that women artists can provide a different service to male artists, and that this is due to gendered behaviour and the capital gained from this.

> I know that I am capable just as any man is, and that my gender does not affect my ability to produce good work. But on the other hand, I will use my femininity to help me with my customer rapport.
>
> YA

Here YA describes actively using her femininity during the tattooing trans-action, and yet it was YA who we saw in the previous chapter describing being advised to 'hold herself' correctly in front of male peers, tone down her femininity and avoid using overly-feminised equipment such as pink machines. Although the overtly 'feminine' symbolic indicators such as pink machines were seen in the last chapter as something to be managed and controlled, emotions – and typically feminine traits – in comparison to pink equipment, for example, are considered valuable and something worth utilising. There is somewhat of a conflict between this displaying of feminised artefacts, described by YA in the previous chapter, and the displaying of feminine qualities to ensure the comfort of the client, described by YA above. This is an interesting conflict: why are women expected to downplay their femininity in some respects, but not in others? Why are some aspects of femininity legitimised and others not? Is there perhaps a difference between 'acting' feminine and 'looking' feminine, and the ways in which this is legitimised?

Overtly feminised equipment is visible, 'out there' and adheres to the notion of a dominant femininity and perhaps this is a difficult concept for the industry, with its dominant norms of masculinity, to accept. Caring, listening and other typically 'feminine' traits, however, are not visible, and can be appropriated and utilised by male artists as well as benefiting the client, and in turn the industry – they are, therefore, often legitimised because this is *useful* appropriation. 'Looking' feminine, however, and buying into overtly feminine-looking equipment, for example, is perhaps *too* visibly feminine, and, therefore, not *useful* and in turn, not legitimised. This is not to say, however, that feminine traits, specifically caring and being attentive, are always appropriated and welcomed by the industry, and we can certainly see in the experiences of IK or NT, for example, that they have both had interactions with men tattoo artists who do not utilise these typically feminine qualities. In fact, they may even argue that some men artists purposefully reject these qualities *because* of their association with the feminine.

In addition to the discussion around useful, authentic capital, the narratives showed that as well as the women describing having to negotiate their own femininities, they actively engaged throughout the interviews in constructing what I saw to be 'acceptable' and 'unacceptable' femininities displayed by fellow women artists. We can link this back to the previous chapter and the discussion around 'othering' artists, but more importantly, it needs to be considered here in the context of the intersections of gender with capital, legitimisation and authenticity.

> Female tattooers use 'selfies' and underwear shots to get as many followers on the internet as possible. I personally would rather people just like my work, however like I say, I'm one of the lads [...]. I follow a lot of female tattooers on Instagram. One in particular, annoyed that many people with her selfies, it caused another female tattooist to comment 'how about you spend your time concentrating on your work...' or something like that. This selfie obsessed tattooist got hundreds of followers every time she put up a flattering picture. Great way to network, but not what I would do. I want to be recognised for my work and music, not my face [...] But then a few well known female tattooists are also models and suicide girls[1]. It does make you wonder if they'd be as well known if they kept their clothes on? I suppose women are empowered by sex, and men love looking at women, and so it's a

---

[1]*Suicide Girls* is an 'alt porn' website, offering an alternative to mainstream online pornography, featuring women who supposedly do not conform to mainstream ideals of femininity or sexual attractiveness (i.e. they might have unnatural hair colours, tattoos, piercings). Not only does it offer an alternative to the aesthetics of mainstream pornography, but the website markets itself on its empowering ethos, maintaining the women featured remain in control of their images and the acts they perform.

great way to promote your work. I just wouldn't feel comfortable, and like I say, I want my work to speak for itself.

KB

Some female artists use their sexuality to promote themselves and their work, rightly or wrongly. They may tattoo in bikinis at conventions, or pose scantily clad for magazines. This gets judged, as it could be seen as selling herself not her art. However, the beautiful female figure is something that the men do not have, why not use it to its full advantage! [...] I think it is very important that a woman is proud to be a female tattoo artist, no matter if they are a tomboy or a girlie girl...However, whilst I do not believe we should not hide from being female, it shouldn't be because we have women's bodies that we stand tall. I do think that women can offer a more approachable service, even perhaps a more delicate, feminine design so it is for these differences we should be honoured in setting our own pathway.

YA

Here we see 'other' women artists being criticised for using their sexuality to promote their work and themselves. Both YA and KB had mentioned in their interviews that the industry is crowded and, therefore, it was important to stand out and be noticed, and that being a woman sometimes helped this. And yet here we see YA and KB openly criticising their fellow artists for attempting to stand out – even identifying that it's a 'great way to network' and 'promote your work', but still condemning the method. I would argue that this constructs parameters in relation to what YA and KB consider to be an acceptable use of femininity and what is unacceptable, or how to *do femininity properly*. YA especially has openly discussed using her femininity to positively influence the rapport between herself and her clients, and to ensure her clients have an enjoyable tattooing experience. However, it seems that using one's femininity (and sexuality) to promote your work is 'unacceptable' and inauthentic. YA states that she does not think a woman should stand out *just* for being a woman. Very much like the use of pink equipment, this *visible* utilisation of femininity is not a legitimate use of femininity; only this time, it is the women who determine this. This creates and reproduces boundaries for the artists to use in distancing themselves from the 'other' artists, as discussed in the previous chapter. By voicing their disapproval of this use of femininity, they are both affirming femininity and distancing themselves from it at the same time, constructing a boundary to establish who is doing femininity properly and who is not. This can also be compared to discussions around Kat Von D in the previous chapter and the ambivalence felt towards the influence she has had upon the status of women in the industry. Both KB and YA have identified as 'one of the boys' previously and so perhaps are comparing these versions of hyper-femininity to the more masculinised identities they relate to (Renold, 2005), constructing their own ideals of what it is to be not only a woman, but more importantly perhaps, a woman tattoo artist. YA discursively constructs the tomboy/girly-girl binary, after previously self-identifying as a tomboy and states that she would, rather her work, speak for itself. KB questions the artist's professionalism and authenticity, and is somewhat disparaging of these 'other' women's work. YA's description of the women who tattoo in bikinis at conventions seems a somewhat exaggerated version of the hyper-feminine woman, and is perhaps part of a narrative in which the 'girly-girl' who engages in this version of femininity is contrived as a symbolic marker of the excesses of 'hegemonic femininity' (Holland and Harpin, 2015:307) and is something for YA to place herself in opposition to.

Dominant norms of femininity and hegemonic gender orders are more likely to shift when women are not isolated in their challenges; if women are able to create spaces independent of masculine-controlled institutions, gendered norms could be deconstructed and reorganised (Finley, 2010; Garrison, 2000; Klein, 1997; Moore, 2007). Just as in the history of feminism, from consciousness-raising groups to the Riot Grrrl movement, networks for the unity of women are critical (Moore, 2007). Women in subcultures and the mainstream, however, often 'distance themselves from what might possibly be their best source of support: other girls' (LeBlanc, 1999:220), especially if they have been isolated from other women because of competition nurtured and encouraged by patriarchy. Negotiations of alternative femininities frequently occur in settings where the overall power of the masculine to define the negotiation overwhelms dynamics between femininities (Finley, 2010:366). As discussed previously, boundaries are created and maintained by and amongst women, which often leads to women policing others' femininities.

The Body Worker and the Body Worked

The engagement and embodiment of emotional labour, seen above in the women's description of the care and attention to their clients' needs, was another way in which the women utilised their feminine capital. It is important now to explore how gendered capital relates to the labour processes involved in both the practice of tattooing and the practice of being the tattooer, and to unpack the complex and interrelated aspects of tattooing as body work and the bodies that carry out this work.

Wolkowitz (2006) explains 'body work' to mean 'employment that takes the body as its immediate site of labour, involving intimate, messy contact with the (frequently supine or naked) body, its orifices or products through touch or close proximity' (Wolkowitz, 2006:147). Wolkowitz explains that the term body work has previously been used to describe the work people do on their own bodies, and she argues for the widening of this description to include the experiences of paid workers whose work involves 'the care, pleasure, adornment, discipline and cure of others' bodies (Wolkowitz, 2006:147).

Research identified by Wolkowitz (Glassner, 1995, Munro, 1999) has found that body workers are often drawn to their occupations via their experiences as consumers in the field, and, therefore, their focus is often on the experience of the consumer rather than them as paid workers (Wolkowitz, 2006:148). This is certainly an aspect within my research, whereby the women focus largely on the experience they can offer the client rather than their own experiences – it is, therefore, important that research projects such as this allow opportunity for the voices of body workers to be heard and explored. We can also see, in the narrative of IK especially, that some of the women were influenced by their own experiences as consumers.

> Many, many clients are referred to me after they have had bad experiences at professional parlours – most women tell stories of being bullied, scoffed at or just simply ignored. I hear these tales over and over, and certainly, when I got the one studio tatt that I have, from a man, that is how I was treated as well.
>
> IK

IK voices the negative experiences she has had with male artists as a consumer and frames this as something that drove her to want to offer a different service to her clients, as Wolkowitz identified in her research on body workers. Wolkowitz criticises previous research on body work or work on the body and states it has focused primarily on emotional labour, thus separating mind and body to the detriment of a full understanding of the situation – by separating emotional work and body work, the understanding of physical care of the body is narrowed (Wolkowitz, 2006:149). Emotional labour should not be equated solely with the mind, but as a practice of the body also. As I progressed through my research, it became increasingly apparent that emotional work could not and should not be considered as separate from body work, and I soon discovered that the exploration of tattooing in this context offers an even more complex set of issues than I had originally anticipated. What makes the discussion difficult is the notion that tattooing is a practice reliant upon the interlocking of not only body work and emotional work, but aesthetics too. And so although Wolkowitz argues for body work and emotional labour to remain interconnected, I am suggesting that we further complexify this by arguing that emotional labour cannot or should not be considered separately from aesthetic labour in the context of creative body work. I specify creative body work as I am not arguing that *all* body work involves the same level of aesthetic commitment that is seen in tattooing. Caring or nursing, for example, would involve different levels of aesthetic labour than creative body work such as tattooing or hairdressing, and there is, I would argue, less of an emphasis on the uniqueness of the body worker in areas such as nursing, for example. The link between the body, emotion work, creativity and the aesthetic must also be explored and acknowledged (Sheane, 2012:147) and was certainly something expressed in the interviews.

> When I get to do a piece I really love or am interested in there is nothing I enjoy more than tattooing. Intricate, delicate work gets me really excited! The moment where people see the finished piece,

and it's a design we've worked hard on together and they really love it is very special too – often they will hug me or get very emotional. There is just a different feeling with some – you get a connection, and it's an intimate space. This usually happens when the piece is something I have worked together with someone – when I just get given an image to copy that rarely happens – which is why I don't enjoy it very much – and why I don't tattoo so much. I prefer to wait until someone seeks me out especially because they want my drawing style.

IK

I love the idea I can be giving other people confidence too through my work. Covering scars and old crappy tattoos, is a very gratifying thing. So many customers are like 'oh I can wear a shoulder-less top' or a bathing suit on holiday just because of a new tattoo. It's amazing!

KB

These quotes illustrate the relationship between body work, emotional labour and the creative process and lead us to further question why previous research has created a binary between mind and body. Wolkowitz equates the relative neglect of the relationship between emotional labour and body work to the fact that much body work is done in private, or at least out of the immediate eye of the public, and so it is difficult to observe without invading the privacy of the client or patient (Wolkowitz, 2006:58). And yet, the moments of bodily contact are often the most significant moments of social contact (Wolkowitz, 2006:58) – this is reflected in the narratives of my participants, who described the personal interactions they have with their clients whilst they tattoo them.

I am a therapist. I have counselled people through so much, and just been that ear that the customer needed for a few hours. I have talked out so many situations with people. It's very important for people to feel like they have a safe place, where they are not judged. I hope that every customer that leaves the studio, feels better about life. By learning about other people's lives, I learn about my own. I've had customers that I've had deep spiritual conversations with, and they've made me think about everything, which actually was pretty depressing! Still, as much as I am there for my customers, I unload a lot too. I love getting people's opinions on aspects of my life. Just talking to people in an intimate environment, means they tell you things they would never tell anyone. After all, I don't know them. I won't judge them. I love being the person they can talk too. It gives me a purpose outside of tattooing, which I love also.

KB

Here KB not only expresses how she is 'therapist' to her clients, but how she feels the interaction is mutually beneficial for both herself and the client. IK's quote above also illustrates her enjoyment of the tattooing process. This offers a different view of emotional labour to previous work – especially that of Hochschild (1983) who suggested that workers learn to develop strategies for 'dealing' with the stress caused by having to manage the self and emotions at work and that workers felt a conflict between their 'true feelings' and the emotions they displayed. This has been since criticised (see Wolkowitz, 2006) and further research has suggested that workers cope with the emotional side of labour better than Hochschild (2003) once argued. This is particularly relevant to my research as the women's narratives present a pride and enjoyment in the emotional labour of tattooing; they do not talk of managing it or feeling burdened by it. The women I interviewed do not see their emotional labour as a performance, or certainly did not express it as such in their interviews. Their narratives showed the importance attached to emotional labour and an emotional investment into the care and positive experience that this offered the client. Of course, I am not denying that there might be times, as with any profession which involves high levels of emotion work, when the tattooer is exposed to stories or experiences that they may find traumatic. However, the artists in the first phase of interviewing only portrayed positive insights into the emotional labour they engaged in and the benefit it had not just for their clients, but also themselves. It was only when I discussed the #tattoometoo movement with artists, that emotional distress was spoken about, and I will address this in the next chapter.

Along with a client's emotional needs, the women spoke about the physical needs of the client during the tattooing process. Emotional labour is fundamental in ensuring the artist provides support for the client through what will be a *physically* painful experience. As with clients' emotions, the artists placed an importance upon this support and linked the management of pain with the client's vulnerability and a lack of power during the process.

> Power imbalance is a huge deal. I think there is an intrinsic imbalance: one person is marked forever; the other person is not. There's no bridging that, but I think many artists want to do their best to ameliorate the effects of that power imbalance on the interaction. I personally don't want anyone to go through with anything they are not one hundred percent down for, and I think that's the fear with the power imbalance: that the client will push themselves, or deny themselves (not asking for a bathroom break, agreeing to design choices that they're not really feeling, etc) so I do my best to invite my clients to be honest with me about what they want and ask for breaks whenever they need them.
>
> LC

I do believe that you put a lot of trust into a tattooist when you get a tattoo. You are in a vulnerable position for a number of reasons:

your health and safety (which is paramount), you're putting trust in the skill of the artist, plus the physical position that you place yourself.

YA

I also like the interaction with interesting clients.

Though it can happen that everyone wants to be my friend afterwards because I've spent three hours causing them pain and they've told me their most secret secrets.

I equate it to torture.

I'm causing them pain and all of a sudden they're spilling their guts.

it's funny.

NT

These quotes illustrate the level of insight the women have into the client experience and how they can work to alleviate feelings of vulnerability, powerlessness and pain. As previously discussed, caring and nurturing are traditionally seen as feminine traits, and so the issue of pain management and overcoming vulnerability may be another reason that clients seek out women artists specifically. There is a complex power dynamic at play: body workers, by the nature of the work they do, are in a position of power in relation to the bodies they are working on, regardless of their status or position within a wider hierarchical context (Wolkowitz, 2006:163). Clients are often in a vulnerable position due to the nature of the transaction. Further to this, women tattooers, as we have seen, have historically been placed in a position of powerlessness within the industry and yet they are able to use their feminine capital to reduce the power imbalance between them and their clients. It may be their femaleness that deems them powerless in the field, but it is their femininity that can break down power imbalances for the benefit of the client.

The women can reflect upon their own experiences as tattoo consumers and empathise with clients, which in turn affects their ability to deploy emotional labour to support the client. The ability and willingness to reflect upon their own experiences in order to improve their actions as tattooers is emotional labour in itself.

Commodifying the Self

The body is, of course, not only a source of labour, but also the product or 'artefact' of labour (Wolkowitz, 2006:27); this is especially relevant for tattoo artists. The body of a tattooer is usually a 'worked on' (Wolkowitz, 2006:27) body as well as a body that 'works on' other bodies and so here we have one example of how aesthetic labour manifests itself for the tattoo artist. However, there are myriad ways in which aesthetic labour presents itself for the tattooer and unpacking these is a complicated task.

Aesthetic labour in the workplace is something previously explored by a number of sociologists (Pettinger, 2010; Warhurst and Nickson, 2007), and when I began to consider the aesthetic labour involved in tattooing, I realised that the aesthetic labour of a tattoo artist in relation to their body is different from the more corporation-focused occupations researched previously (Witz et al., 2003). Whereas in previous research, aesthetic labour usually involves an expectation on the workforce to look a certain way to 'fit in' with company policy, or to attract clients or customers, the dynamics for the tattooer differs to this. The tattooer works for themselves primarily, and so any 'labour' they partake in is to, ultimately, benefit themselves (and to a lesser extent the studio they work in). However, what the narratives suggest is that the pressure and expectation to look at certain way comes from the members of the sub-culture, clients and potential clients. Therefore, in order to understand and explore the aesthetic labour undertaken by the tattooer, we need to shift the focus from the employer–worker relationship to that of the worker–customer relationship (Sheane, 2012:146).

> Another element of being a tattooist that is up for judgement is how many tattoos we wear ourselves. I believe it is expected of us to be a walking canvas of our trade. The public tend to want to see that the professional they are seeking has an interest in their profession, for instance a mechanic who drives a car or a hairdresser with a stylish haircut. I have worked with a tattooist who had no tattoos, and she often was questioned on why she had no ink yet would tattoo people every day.
>
> YA

> I think I mentioned before that customers in the shop would downright ignore me when I didn't have visible tattoos. Some even commented that that was grounds for not trusting me...I'm on the fence with this one. I do think every tattooer should have at least a few...so they know what they are doing to people you know? So that they have been on both sides. But I still think it is unfair to judge an artist's work based on the tattoos they have...it's just silly
>
> AA

> Almost every person I tattoo who doesn't know me comments on it [IK's lack of visible tattoos] – I think it makes some of them nervous as they may not know how long I have been tattooing for, and they are too shy to ask if I'm new to it.
>
> IK

The narratives illustrate the pressure felt by artists and the expectation that potential clients have for their tattooist to be tattooed themselves. For the tattooist, the tattooed body is a symbol of professionalism and authenticity, and maybe even of devotion to the industry. As AA states, an un-tattooed body may even be grounds for not trusting the artist. IK also alludes to the idea that a tattooed body is an indicator of the artist's ability – which, of course, in reality it cannot be, and, therefore, the tattooed body acts somehow as a symbolic indicator of ability. AA makes the link between aesthetic and emotional labour, suggesting that artists who are tattooed can show empathy towards clients who are getting tattooed. This echoes my previous suggestion that the women were themselves reflecting upon their experiences of being tattooed for them to provide a better service for the client. We can begin to see from these quotes how the level of aesthetic labour employed by the artists might influence the economic capital gained. Research conducted by Entwistle and Wissinger (2006) on the modelling industry and the aesthetic labour employed by the models in the field shows that although it is a very different field from that of tattooing, the employment of aesthetic labour holds similarities to the narratives in my own research. The research identifies models as being 'freelancers' rather than employees of organisations or corporations. It suggests that the pressures of aesthetic labour impacts upon freelance workers differently, because, like tattooers, it is themselves that models are marketing and commodifying; they are the product to promote (Entwistle and Wissinger, 2006:776), as illustrated here:

> ...workers seeking employment in aesthetic industries or occupations might also come to see their bodies as the 'hardware' and perform aesthetic labour to gain/maintain employment.
>
> (Entwistle and Wissinger, 2006:781)

Ashley Mears (2011) talks about models as being part of a 'growing workforce of "aesthetic labourers", those workers whose bodies and personalities – the "whole person" – are up for purchase on the market' (Mears, 2011:13). Although the tattooist is not commodifying themselves to the extent seen by the fashion model – in which their *actual* body is the promoted product – the tattooist is similarly promoting their work, their trade and themselves as body workers, and their physical appearance is likely to influence people's perceptions of them. As the quotes above suggest, displaying their tattooed bodies in the 'right' way has a significant effect upon their ability to gain work within the sub-culture. The tattoos displayed on their bodies do not necessarily indicate the quality of their own work as tattooists because usually they were made by other artists, but as the participant quotes above show, heavy coverage still promotes in clients a feeling of professionalism and authenticity. This suggests that *aesthetic capital* in the field of tattooing is another influential form of capital, one which relates to what Thornton would term 'objective capital' (1995:11). As previously discussed, objective capital can be displayed through books and art (Thornton, 1995:11), for example, and so would include aesthetics, however aesthetics refers specifically to 'the look' and is also linked to professionalism and authenticity.

This illustrates a link between aesthetic labour, aesthetic capital and the subsequent conversion to economic capital. We can further relate this to gendered capital by exploring how these factors influence the women's ability to promote their business and make money – just as the models who promote themselves might do. Wolkowitz argues that some employers in the service sector choose to employ women in order to use their gender and (hetero) sexuality to increase profits by appealing to and pleasing male customers (Wolkowitz, 2006:81). The focus is on the utilisation of gendered capital to appeal to the male gaze, gratifying male customers who subsequently spend their money, aiding the conversion of gendered capital into economic capital. The use of female capital in the tattoo industry can be considered in some ways as contrary to this. What the participants suggest is that women artists manage, utilise and employ their own versions of female capital to appeal to clients, thus increasing their own economic capital at the same time as providing a women-led service to their women clients, ultimately resulting in female capital benefiting women on both 'sides' of the 'transaction'. This is an empowering position for the women artists, and the clients, to be in, but also relies heavily on the women engaging in the 'right' amount of aesthetic labour for this gendered capital to be useful, and readily converted into financial success.

> The client leaves with this lovely shiny exciting cool new tattoo and spends the next days showing and telling everyone about their tattoo and tattooist.
>
> Then prospective clients come in asking for so and so that did so and so's tattoo, so then you're in demand and….you know...that sort of thing.
>
> NT

> I think the main reason my clients are mostly female, is because women talk. I've had a few customers that are really glad that they are getting tattooed by a female, but then obviously they tell their friends, who are also female and it goes on from there. In saying that, as a woman, it's much easier to be in an intimate position with another female, than a strange man.
>
> KB

Both KB and NT recognise that their client base and reputation are built from 'word of mouth' publicity – if women clients have a positive experience with a woman artist, the way in which subcultures and sub-cultures are structured and organised mean that it is likely that the client will share her experiences with other members of the subculture or community. There is a strength in this that does not exist in fields such as management or caring as discussed above, and this is due to the nature of the gendered capital and how it operates in the sub-cultural field of tattooing. Women artists do not necessarily have to rely on other (male) artists to succeed in the industry and can manage themselves as independent agents in the field, especially with social media platforms such as Instagram being used so readily. Wolkowitz argues that the body work enabling the (re)making of bodies often goes unrecognised in relation to who carried out the work – the 'wearer' of the body work is credited with the cultural capital it produces and yet the body worker is not (Wolkowitz, 2006:168). This, however, is generally not the case for tattoo artists who often get credited for their work – within subcultures, it is common practice for fellow tattooed individuals to ask who did 'your work' and it is indeed how artists gain a prospective client base, as illustrated in both NT and KB's quotes above.

To manage and maintain levels of capital, however, requires a degree of investment – both in terms of time and emotions. Entwistle and Wissinger describe how this degree of aesthetic labour can lead to the feeling of always 'being on' – finding it difficult to break from work, as the body is always a performance of the commodified self (Entwistle and Wissinger, 2006:791). Freelance work does not allow for a complete separation between work self and private self and is often reliant upon the projection of 'personality' (Entwistle and Wissinger, 2006:787). We have already seen evidence of this throughout the narratives – in the previous chapter where women describe being approached when outside of work, and above where KB and NT discuss how business is promoted throughout the community via 'word of mouth'. This suggests that aesthetic labour includes and extends emotional labour (Entwistle and Wissinger, 2006:791) and further proves that they should not be considered as independent from each other in the context of tattooing.

> I've come to the conclusion that tattooing is more than a career for several reasons, it is a lifestyle. You can't really separate yourself from it if you want to be really successful. You work round the clock bringing in new clientele, drawing appointments, painting flash sets[2] . . .I think I've found a way to be okay with that and now the struggle is to keep my own art separate from work so that it stays alive.
>
> AA

AA identifies here that tattooing is a lifestyle rather than a career, which further demonstrates the feeling of being 'always on' identified by Entwistle and Wissinger (2006) of freelance workers. As well as the labour of promoting business, there is the physical labour of preparing for appointments. With social media becoming such a crucial part of promoting business, aesthetic labour is also

---

[2]'Flash sets' are sheets of designs drawn up by artists for clients to choose from. These sets are often displayed in studios for customers to browse, rather than having a custom design drawn up specifically for them by the artist.

performed via the internet in the promoting of the artist and their work. This also increases the merging of work and leisure, and the feeling that the artist is never truly away from their work (Hracs and Leslie, 2014:66).

> There is a massive expectation from some people of the service we provide. Almost like we're not human. I spend all evening drawing, re-drawing or answering messages. If someone cancels their appointment at the last minute, we have to try and find a replacement appointment to fill the spot. I often get messages that literally just say "?????" – chasing me up after they sent a message, and I didn't reply immediately.
>
> KB

KB demonstrates how difficult it is for artists to leave their work in the workplace and the pressure they feel from customers. KB, who in the interviews compared the service she provided to therapy for her clients, exposes here how difficult this service is to sustain. Artists put themselves under pressure to provide a service to their clients whilst at home as well as at work. However, making attempts to manage this, and perhaps *not* answering messages from home, risks losing clients and, therefore, decreasing economic capital.

Managing the Self

Aesthetic labour is, of course, also performed on a day-to-day basis in the tattooing transaction between artists and client:

> In terms of presenting to clients I like to look smart and non-intimidating.
>
> That's because so many of my clients talk about how intimidating going in to a tattoo studio can be.
>
> NT

> However you present yourself as a tattooer with the style you chose to wear, makes a difference to how you will be perceived by some. Others won't notice. Again, I believe this is the same within so many careers and industries. I wear what I feel comfortable in, as I need to be at ease when I work. Although I do not really consider 'the customer's opinion on the choice of my clothes/hair etc, I will make sure that I am always tidy in my appearance, clean and sweet smelling, as I am a professional in my industry and I have to make sure that comes across.
>
> YA

This quote from NT illustrates just how aesthetic and emotional labour are intrinsically linked and how the artists themselves navigate this. NT actively makes choices about her clothing and the way in which she presents herself to meet the emotional needs of her clients. YA, too, is aware of the level of aesthetic labour she engages in, although unlike NT, she does not consider her customers' opinions in her choice of clothing. However, YA does link her aesthetic labour with her level of professionalism and wants this to come across to clients. Interestingly, YA also likens this labour to other forms of employment – even though in the previous chapter, YA was one of the artists who distanced tattooing from 'other' forms of employment, arguing that tattooing allowed for greater freedom in the workplace. This suggests once again that there is a degree of negotiation and fluidity within the tattooing field. On the one hand, the industry allows playfulness and freedom, but on the other hand, the industry – just like any other industry – has its own unwritten 'rules' to which the artists adhere. Perhaps these unwritten rules are also experienced by men artists. If these pressures are coming from inside of the community in general – meaning tattoo consumers – perhaps the masculine ideal of the rock star image that seems so entrenched in the narratives of the women is one that the men artists feel they too must live up to.

IK was the first artist I interviewed, to talk about the environment in which she tattoos, and I put this down to the fact she is the only interviewee to tattoo from her home. Interestingly, IK's narrative identifies yet another source of aesthetic labour, in the setting up and management of the tattooing milieu:

> The main difference I could see that probably exists is that I set up a calm, inviting space which is rather aesthetic. I play calming music and I dress normally – also I tattoo from my house. So someone coming to me is having a very, very different experience from a parlour, where the vibe is often incredibly macho and intimidating. Tattooists seem often to enjoy propagating the stereotype of themselves as tough or scary – aligning with 'metal' culture, which also goes along with piercing. I'm not against that vibe, it is just not what I like to work within. If I worked in a shop I would find that very stressful, and to be honest it is one of the main reasons I haven't ever looked for work as a professional, even though my skill level is adequate – I try to avoid places in general where I feel I might be threatened or treated poorly because it a male dominated environment – so I suppose in that way gender is something which definitely effects my practice.
>
> IK

Here we see IK's attention to detail such as music, atmosphere and clothing. I did ask IK to explain her use of the term 'dressing normally', as she had previously told me that she dressed rather alternatively, with what might be deemed an alternative hairstyle. IK wanted to emphasise that she purposefully did not dress in an intimidating manner, and as we can see from the quote above, it is important for IK to set up an environment different to those she herself and her clients have experienced. IK invests a lot of emotion and time in the constructing and creating of the environment to give her clients a positive experience – further illustrating the intertwining of both emotional and aesthetic labour.

Aesthetic labour is also used in the management of stigma attached to the profession, although there is a paradox at the centre of this stigma management. Having a tattooed body holds capital in the sub-culture, and because of their tattoos, the tattooer is taken more seriously as an artist. However, at the same time, on the outside of the community, artists who are heavily tattooed are often in a position of having to manage stigma attached to heavy tattoo coverage. There is, therefore, an amount of labour that goes into negotiating and managing any public display of the body. This relates to the discussion in the previous chapter around the tensions between internal and external sub-cultural capital – the capital held by tattooists outside of the community is different from that held inside the community. Labour is employed in the attempt to manage the way in which people see heavily tattooed people and/or tattooers.

> I feel my role is to demonstrate that we aren't all drug addicted felons really. That we are normal people who just choose to do tattoos for a living.
>
> AA

> I'd like to think that this [the increase in women in the industry] is having a positive impact on society, particularly people who will never have a tattoo. The people who would usually look down their noses at a woman covered in tattoos, or think that only criminals have ink, maybe they will begin to change their opinions slightly once they meet these hugely welcoming, peaceful women who just so happen to have beautiful artwork etched in their skin.
>
> YA

The need to challenge the stigma attached to being a tattooed woman, and a woman tattooer, is expressed here by both YA and AA; they suggest this to be a very prominent factor in their embodied identity and daily experiences as a tattoo artist. Previous research on tattooed women, as discussed in Chapter 2, explored the stigma attached to the tattooed woman's body and how the norms and ideals of femininity in mainstream society affect the way tattooed bodies are viewed (Atkinson, 2002; Dann, 2021; Pitts, 2003). Heavily tattooed women artists, therefore, are placed in a context whereby they are constantly negotiating their own versions of femininity with society's versions of femininity. This is further complicated by having also to negotiate the gendered capital they hold *within* the tattooed community, which is sometimes conflicting with public perception. The way in which women tattooers are viewed, therefore, is in constant flux and tension, between being stigmatised and wanting to challenge these perceptions, to being highly regarded and awarded capital and status.

The women interviewed want to take an active role in positively affecting the non-tattooed public's perception of tattooed people and tattooers. The tattoo artist has historically been linked to the association with marginal and deviant groups, and, therefore, has held negative connotations (Adams, 2012:150). The role of the tattooer could therefore, as Adams (2012) suggests, be deemed 'deviant labour' which entails what he calls, 'dirty work' (2012:150). Adams links cosmetic surgery and tattooing and explains that both industries specialise in the modification of the body with varying degrees of social acceptability (2012:150) and although both began as 'disreputable fields', both have achieved new levels of acceptability. Practitioners in both industries, Adams argues, have worked on renovating their images in the eyes of the mainstream public (Adams, 2012:149), wanting to legitimise their work and the fields/industries in which they make their living.

Adams argues, then, that both the tattoo and cosmetic surgery industries could be considered physically, socially and morally tainted industries – stigmatised and discredited based upon their public perception and the nature of the work (Adams, 2012:152). However, this is in stark contrast to how tattoo artists are respected and granted capital within the tattoo community. As I have discussed, with the growing television coverage and celebrity endorsement, the tattoo artist is no longer always seen as deviant or discredited. This change in attitude towards artists is not entirely down to television and media, however, and as YA and AA's quotes suggest, there are still many in mainstream society who do discredit the role of the tattooer, which means artists are engaging in aesthetic and emotional labour, such 'therapeutic' work with their clients, to challenge and change these public perceptions. We can perhaps understand the importance of challenging these perceptions when we consider the level of embodiment and emotional investment in tattooing work and, as discussed above, the feeling of being 'always on' – if tattoos or tattooing is criticised, it is not just the act of tattooing under scrutiny, but the embodied self of the artist also.

Conclusion

In contrast to the previous chapter, this chapter explores femininity as something to be positively utilised by participants to gain capital, status and career advancement and satisfaction. Femaleness and femininity are considered here as forms of embodied cultural capital, in relation to body work and emotional labour. Although in the previous chapter, being a woman was identified as a barrier to entry to the tattoo industry, this chapter illustrates how once in the industry, being a woman and utilising gendered capital can, in some ways, aid one's position in the field. The chapter looks at women tattooists' experiences of being a body worker, and what being a woman (or utilising traits associated with femininity) can bring to the body worker/body worked relationship.

The participants took pride in the way in which their femininity was employed to provide a better service to their clients, and this, in turn, has the potential to disrupt the dominance of the hegemonic masculinity experienced as intimidating, oppressive and constraining by many individuals within tattoo culture.

Women actively negotiate and navigate between levels of femininity in their daily experience of being a woman artist in a male-dominated sub-culture and industry. Whereas the previous chapter discussed downplaying the aesthetic qualities of dominant femininities, this chapter highlights the conflict between *looking* feminine and *acting* in a feminine way, and yet remaining 'tough' enough to survive a male-dominated industry. There appears to be acceptable and unacceptable performances of femininity, underpinned by notions of alternative versus hegemonic gender norms. In the previous chapter, I discussed how artists 'other' fellow artists, and this discussion is continued in this chapter, where participants appeared to be constructing their own boundaries surrounding 'right' and 'wrong' demonstrations and uses of femininity.

The capital held by the artist, therefore, is fluid and paradoxical in its nature and the artist cannot always predict if this capital will be useful, or if this capital will be meaningless in any particular setting or interaction. On the one hand, television and media coverage has increased the tattoo artist's capital amongst those who take an interest in tattooing. However, for those with a more negative view of tattoos and tattooing, the artists hold no capital and they are placed in a position of having to manage and negotiate public perception and possible stigma. Workers within once deviant industries have had to strive to achieve social legitimacy, using both emotional and aesthetic labour, to enable the industries to grow and reduce the stigma within the mainstream (Adams, 2012: 152).

Adams argues that it is important, in legitimising 'deviant' industries, that they are 'reframed' from potentially deviant cultural practices and focus is drawn to the 'non stigmatized aspects of the work' (Adams, 2012:158). By focusing upon the care and 'therapy' that artists provide for their clients, and how they present themselves in public, outside of the community, the industry begins to be legitimised. Emotional labour is also used in legitimising the self; it can also be used discursively as a way of reinforcing the body worker's sense of self as a professional and not 'just' a tattooer (Gimlin, 1996) – thus, not only legitimising the profession to the wider society, but on a more personal level also.

In this chapter, I have highlighted the inextricable, interrelationship between body work, emotional labour and aesthetic labour. Contrary to previous research on emotional labour (Hochschild, 1983), my research shows that emotional labour can be beneficial for both the worker and the recipient, and the participants alluded to their emotional labour as embodied rather than a purposeful and/ or isolated performance. Emotional labour is also employed in the management of stigma associated with tattooing. Participants demonstrated how important aesthetic labour is in the tattoo industry, and although different from more organisational or corporation-based labour, tattooing retains a link between commodifying the self and increasing economic capital, at the same time as being used to manage stigma, much like emotional labour. A downside to the types of labour and the investment and commitment to the labour discussed throughout the chapter is the feeling of always 'being on'; this has increased with the popularity of social media to promote the work of tattooists and leads to a lack of distance between a home self and work self, which is something that the women artists have to manage both professionally and personally often with more constraints and pressures then men artists, who are less likely to be primary caregivers.

The next chapter will further explore the utilisation of gendered capital, but rather than put the emphasis on how artists manage and negotiate the existing sub-culture, I want to acknowledge their attempts to create and change the industry and sub-culture.

Chapter 5

Resisting, Reframing and Rethinking the Tattoo Industry

As noted in previous chapters, many of the artists I spoke to described their use of tattoos and tattooing to resist and subvert mainstream culture after feeling pressure to conform; and we know that tattoos are used to challenge mainstream femininity and the hegemonic western ideals placed upon women by society (Dann, 2018, 2021). However, if subcultures are the vehicle through which a resistance to the mainstream is constructed, what happens when the internal structure of the sub-culture is what requires resistance? When faced with a community and industry steeped in hegemonic masculine norms and values, many women, non-binary and queer artists feel they need to resist these dominant structures from *within* the sub-culture as well as the norms and values of mainstream culture.

To re-conceptualise resistance both politically and theoretically, LeBlanc (1999) argues that we need to explore subjective and objective accounts of resistance, studying not only acts of resistance but the motives behind these acts (LeBlanc, 1999: 17–18). She describes three distinct moments in the act of resistance:

> ... a subjective account of oppression (real or imagined), an express desire to counter that oppression, an action (broadly defined as word, thought or deed) intended specifically to counter that oppression.
>
> (LeBlanc, 1999:18)

With specific focus on 'moments in the act of resistance', this chapter seeks to explore how women and queer tattoo artists are resisting hegemonic gender inequalities, intervening in the masculinised culture of the industry, and attempting to reframe these cultural norms. By connecting themes and discussions from previous chapters I highlight how women and queer artists are utilising their position within the industry, to make the world of tattooing a more welcoming space for people who do not 'fit' within the hegemonic masculine construction of the sub-culture and challenging the people who have (problematically) fit for too long without challenge. I also illustrate how women artists are using their position and platforms to raise awareness of sexist and abusive practices within the

Tattooing and the Gender Turn, 83–108
Copyright © 2023 Emma Beckett
Published under exclusive licence by Emerald Publishing Limited
doi:10.1108/978-1-80262-301-720231005

industry and are championing change. Women may not yet have equal numbers in the industry, but the impact they have made and continue to make is hugely significant (Thompson, 2015:150).

Resistance in Action: Changing Spaces

> Safer spaces... can be understood as *simultaneously* sites of personal safety ('being') and political action ('doing').
>
> (Lohman, 2022:4)

Tattooists of the new generation are creating studios that are very different to those of times gone by, and women seem to be at the forefront of this change (Thompson, 2015:129). The space in which the tattoo is created is becoming more of a focus for academic interrogation, although research with this sole focus is still quite scarce; Modesti (2008) refers to tattoo studios as 'postmodern spaces of agency' and Lane (2021) discusses social stratification, and the organisation of labour across different tattoo spaces, using the hierarchy between artists and apprentices as an example (2021:40–47). The space and the studio will impact greatly on both the client and the artist – as we have seen in previous chapters, many artists have worked in studios they have not felt comfortable or happy in. The studio atmosphere, who works there and how the studio operates, all make a difference to how the client feels when they are getting tattooed, and how the artist feels whilst tattooing. This element of studio management seems to have become increasingly important for many artists, with a specific focus on promoting a friendly and approachable service for clients; using platforms such as Instagram, artists are not only posting photos of the tattoo created, but the space in which the tattoo is made – including information in their 'bios' such as 'feminist tattoo studio' or 'queer-friendly studio'. There has been a significant increase over the last decade of all-women, and queer studios – studios that pride themselves on being inclusive and safe spaces. Even though tattoo has a long history and association with queer culture and politics (DeMello, 2000; Klesse, 2007; Pitts, 2003, 2005), finding an inclusive, queer-friendly, woman-friendly space (for both clients and artists) amidst the more hegemonic masculine spaces has not always been easy.

> I am lucky to have pretty effectively avoided the sexism of the industry by only working for women, and pretty much only working with women. It is a huge relief because I was afraid that I would not be able to learn because a lot of people believe you have to be friends with dudes to learn anything. This is super untrue. I have learned tremendous skill from women, women have taught me to do fine line technical soft grey watercolour effects, things that many people would tell you can't be done.
>
> LC

Here LC illustrates how all-women/queer studios have the potential to become sub-cultural spaces of resistance. By learning from women, LC and their mentors are breaking down the male-centred sub-cultural gatekeeping discussed in previous chapters, creating spaces for themselves and for other artists as they go. The effect of this on the clients and community will be significant also – as we can see below, being genderqueer and a feminist was an integral and influential part of LC's identity as a tattoo artist and fundamental to LC's practice:

> I have had a number of trans and genderqueer clients. Also tattooing in [this area] put me in touch with a lot of queer people of color, and this has been wonderful to me because I want to be in service to queer people, disabled people, genderqueer people, and people of color. These intersectional experiences of oppression can make it hard for clients to want to be vulnerable, be undressed, etc. in a tattoo setting, so I feel lucky that I have worked in shops that are designed to serve marginalized people as well.
>
> LC

> We get lots of LBGTQIA+ clients and I tend to particularly get lots of non-binary and trans clients which I am so honoured to serve. Especially if they haven't had the surgeries they need to be comfortable I take extra care with working with them to make them feel safe. I will never touch without permission nor will I take photos without consent. I'll also go through their plans for surgery just in case it effects the tattoo... Some clients of mine are trans people who have just started their transition and it can be the only time they can be fully open about what they're going through. I absolutely love it. I try to get them involved with the community in the city so they can have friends like them. Some of my clients are well seasoned trans people and I get lots of info from them too. Our little studio community is perfect.
>
> NR

Here NR highlights how important the tattoo space is for the clients and echoes the narratives discussed in Chapter 4, highlighting not only the inclusive nature of NR's studio, but the emotional labour they invest in to ensure their clients – especially those from minority groups – are safe and comfortable. Being a trans person in today's political climate is at the very least, scary and at worst, dangerous. Trans people regularly experience high levels of discrimination, and violence, leading to concerns for their own and their community's safety – this also, unsurprisingly, has significant effects on mental and physical health (Veldhuis et al., 2018). Safe spaces are vital for the emotional and physical safety of all trans people, and although services are improving, actual safe spaces are still scarce. Research has shown that online spaces rather than space *in real life* (Austin et al., 2020) are often used as spaces to share experiences, offer and receive support from peers and communicate safely with members of the trans community. What NR demonstrates here is that inclusive, women or queer-run tattoo studios have the potential and opportunity to offer that safe space in real life. Tattoo studios are often places where people congregate and 'hang out' even if they're not getting tattooed. These have historically been quite masculine spaces, and now artists like NR are working hard to build safe and inclusive communities around their studios. NR also notes here that they 'love' nurturing this community, suggesting, as discussed in previous chapters, that they also benefit from the labour put into this exchange.

> We get lots of comments from our clients especially newbies on how safe we made them feel, how chill our studio is (I'm not allowed to play my angry mental music haha). I also get many clients contacting me tell me that their friend had recommended me for my gentleness and kind studio. The fact they keep coming back and tell their friends is proof enough we're doing a good job.
>
> NR

Here we see that artists can utilise *Queer Capital* (Kjaran and Jóhannesson, 2016) to gain status and standing within a tattoo community that has been longing for a change. At last, queer-friendly studios can run in a way that is counter to the hegemonic masculinised studios we have become accustomed to. Queer-friendly studios can overcome their subordinate position (Kjaran and Jóhannesson, 2016:54) and create something new, inclusive and welcoming, existing and thriving within the industry and not merely on the peripheries of it.

As well as being inclusive and creating a safe space, tattoo studios must still make a profit. If LGBTQ+ clients return to the studio, and tell their peers about the studio, this has a positive financial impact upon the studio also, and although I acknowledge that this was not the point NR was making, it is an important aspect of running a successful tattoo studio. In Chapter 3, I discussed how sub-cultural capital can be 'converted' into economic capital, and although this is not the *only* 'useful' manifestation of capital, it certainly helps in running a business.

> Of course, there are some people in the industry that are still holding on to the macho "traditional" culture but they won't last long. Our job needs to be compassionate because people are putting so much trust in us and our clients can see that.
>
> NR

> I think the macho tattoo culture will shift - so many women are getting into tattooing, and a lot of shops are opening that are all women, or directly aimed at women. I think it's a great thing.

Anything that allows women to feel safer, supported and appreciated is fully endorsed by me.

IK

It is telling that both NR and IK use the term 'macho' here – as we have seen throughout this book, there is a common language between artists who have experienced the male-dominated culture of the tattoo industry. All-women and queer-friendly studios, therefore, have the potential to be the site of resistance for artists working in the studio, at the same time as offering opportunities for tattoo consumers to avoid and resist the more traditional all-male studios some consumers have previously found problematic. As IK identifies here, women, trans and queer folk – both artists and clients – may feel safer, supported and appreciated in these alternative tattooing environments. Adopting a literal interpretation of riot grrrl's 'Girls to the Front' ethos[1] (Marcus, 2010), the increase in all-women tattoo studios show-casing women's artwork, drives women to the forefront of a formally male-centred culture, not only showcasing women's work but encouraging women in their transition from consumer to producer. All-women and queer-friendly spaces help to subvert and challenge the dominant gender norms of the tattoo community and attempt to question, challenge and disrupt the dominance of male artists within the industry.

There is still work to be done, however and although LC celebrates their studio for its inclusionary ethos, they also criticise it for its inherent whiteness. LC identifies as mixed Arab gender queer, and as I discussed in Chapter 4, was the only participant in the first phase of interviews, to discuss race and racism.

I think being Arab gives me a really clear stake in racial justice. I think because I have passing privilege, enjoying the benefits of whiteness in the United States, I am aware that if my skin was darker or if there were other indications of my Arab-ness I would encounter many more barriers. I have seen a dear friend of mine who is an African American artist have to fight against bizarre underestimation and negligence from white male mentors, so I know what this industry does to women of color who are trying to attain skill tattooing. Many women of color who are tattoo artists are powerfully discouraged by people who are in a position to help them achieve what they want. I think many women of color, and many women artists internalize messages that their work is inadequate, so the people who do work tattooing have survived a number of trials. In my own experience, feelings of self doubt, inadequacy and fraudulence feel related to a mixed race identity. A lot of mixed race people are confused about who they are vs. how

---

[1]'Girls to the front' was both a slogan and ethos to live by for riot grrrls – meaning that girls should be allowed, and encouraged to enjoy gigs and concerts from the front of the venue, in a safe space created by the band. It offered an alternative to what girls were usually accustomed to – being pushed and shoved at the back of gigs by the men in attendance.

people perceive us, don't feel we fit in, feel like we're the "only one" like us.

LC

I told LC they were the only participant to address race in the (first phase of) interviews, to which they responded:

> That's too bad no one else is talking about race! I think finding a way to make the practice of tattooing less racist is the absolute most urgent development called for in tattooing. There are a lot of amazing artists of color making work, including very talented women, but it seems like the industry is deeply segregated.

LC

LC offers invaluable insight into the dynamics of race, racism and whiteness within the industry. LC describes their 'passing privileges' and says that because of this, they have not experienced the level of race-related prejudice their friends have. LC also shared with me an essay they wrote, 'calling out' an individual tattoo artist for tattooing a racist image and describes how they challenged a tattoo magazine for printing the 'most racist image I have ever seen in print', for which they received an apology from the editors. The essay discusses the prevalence of racist and culturally appropriative imagery in tattooing, and how very often these images are disguised as Americana nostalgia. LC also calls to artists to create open and welcoming studios for people of colour, and argues that artists need to work on changing the industry to become a better place for people of colour. LC is a good example of how some artists are engaging in activism within the industry, and how this has the potential to instigate and encourage change within tattoo culture.

Instagram, as I have discussed in previous chapters and will discuss further below, has fast become a platform for campaigning and calling out problematic and discriminatory aspects of the industry. There has been a rise in tattoo artists using their accounts or creating accounts to not only highlight the issue of racism within and across tattooing, but as a platform to encourage action against racism, and call for anti-racist tattooing practices.

> [the industry] is still struggling with prejudice... but with the Black Lives Matter movement, which happened around the same time as the metoo movement in tattooing, and the Shades Initiative that was set up to support artists of colour... it's raising awareness of what we need to do better in and hopefully is making an impact, but we've still got a long way to go.

TL

Shades Tattoo Initiative (@shades_tattoo_initiative) was created as a safe space and community to showcase the work of people of colour tattoo artists. They post photos of tattoos by people of colour artists, and information raising awareness of racism and racist practice in the industry. This also highlights, as I did in Chapter 1, the need for further scholarship on the ingrained and systematic racism within the tattoo industry and how this might be addressed by artists' activism. World-wide campaigns such as Black Lives Matter – a campaign founded in 2013 to raise awareness of racism and violence inflicted on black communities – are being embraced by some sections of the tattoo community and as TL argues here, impactful work is being done but the industry has a long way to go. We, as social researchers, could be playing our part in this and as I have discussed previously, I would be very excited to see somebody build upon this work.

Tattoo Conventions

Another strategy for disruption, although one less frequent than all-women and queer-friendly studios, is all-women tattoo conventions.[2] Tattoo conventions are specialised events, with a festival-like atmosphere, held typically over a day or a weekend, to showcase artists, trade stalls and entertainment. DeMello (2000), in her ethnography of the tattoo community, discusses tattoo conventions and the carnivalesque environment they embody. She describes conventions as reflecting the values and politics of Bakhtin's carnival: rowdy, bawdy and liberating spaces – where high culture is debased and dominant social order is subverted (DeMello, 2000:30). This can certainly be applied to many tattoo conventions, which create a micro-environment allowing tattoo enthusiasts to join in a shared interest without mainstream pressures to conform to societal norms. Tattoos are created, looked at, shared and bodies are displayed in a manner that they perhaps would not be in everyday interactions. An all-women convention, therefore, could be considered as a space in which women artists can work, network and showcase their art in a safe and supportive environment.

DS, who worked the first UK female-artist only convention in Royal Leamington Spa (UK), talks about her experience:

> I was approached by [the organiser] and I thought it was a great idea – what a brilliant way of show-casing some of the amazingly talented women who have entered the industry over the last few years. It was good to have a space that was especially for women artists after all this time.
>
> DS

HS, in her interview however, expressed ambivalence towards all-women shows:

> I can remember, probably back in the late 90's, being told about a female-only tattoo convention in the states, and everybody said

---

[2]All-women conventions are conventions that showcase only women artists – customers of all genders are welcome to attend.

isn't that a great idea? And I actually thought no, I don't think it is. My argument wasn't so much that, well, I could see the positives, but my argument was that how would I feel if suddenly there was a male-only convention. To me, it wasn't about empowering, but suddenly if you're excluding, that's taking away... the whole point to me has always been to be equal, so to suddenly segregate, it didn't make me feel comfortable [...] I suppose I can see both sides of the argument, but I didn't want to be segregated, I wanted to be a part of the whole thing. I like that there are more women artists at the shows, that's absolutely fantastic, that is brilliant, but I don't feel I need my own separate show. But that's just me personally, I don't have a problem with other women choosing to work these shows. It's just there are male artists whose work I am inspired by that I want to see. I've heard lots of people say lots of positive things about it, there was a nice atmosphere but I think you get that anywhere.

HS

On the one hand, HS likes that there are more women working conventions; however, she does not feel that women need or should want a separate event. There was mixed views and indecision around conventions from many of the participants: some women had not worked them, but held negative views towards them; others had worked them and not enjoyed them, and some had enjoyed working them.

Maybe I'd go to an international show and take my daughter.

I'd like to take her to a show, but it's finding one that I think is appropriate for her.

Some of them are over 18, some of them have things are just down-right inappropriate. I mean, they say burlesque show, be honest, it's a stripper. Be honest!! [...] It goes back [to] the sexist days, you're a female artist, working the show, and there's a stripper on the stage. Why is it any different? Just because it's deemed arty, and therefore empowering – I'm sure the women back then felt empowered, they were getting paid. Or pick different entertainment; don't alienate certain types of people.

HS

Here HS highlights an interesting conflict when considering conventions. Traditionally, convention entertainment includes performances such as burlesque and/or fire performances (usually performed by women). HS references conventions in general, and how having such performances could alienate many of the potential clients and visitors to the show. One might expect an all-women convention to attempt to provide a different level or type of entertainment, and yet when I attended the first all-women show in Royal Leamington Spa in 2011, part of the entertainment there was made up of burlesque performances and the show was indeed, an over-18 event.[3] Burlesque does have a long-standing association with the world of tattoo – not only are burlesque performers often tattooed, but there is also a pocket of the tattoo community who cross-over into the vintage and pin-up subculture. And so, it is not unusual to see burlesque and pin-up type performances at tattoo events. However, I do think there are conversations to be had around how this could be seen as the commodification of women's bodies in a typically masculine space, and how this could alienate some members of the community. I also acknowledge, however, that this is a complex and nuanced issue that needs time and space for further exploration, outside of this book.

Another significant consideration surrounding all-women conventions was the choice of judges for the show competitions. At the convention I attended, the competitions were judged by three male judges. This highlights the complex issues at play with what is framed as a women-centred space. I would suggest that the use of men judges in an all-women show is problematic. It brings into question gendered power and hierarchies, mirroring and perpetuating the previously explored notion that being a male artist equates to an authenticity and legitimised knowledge of the industry and undermines both the need for a women-only convention, and that women artists should be 'taken seriously'. Halberstam (2003) suggests that subcultures are often objects of voyeurism – with this in mind, the women-only convention that places men in the powerful position of judging the artist's work could be seen as merely creating the convention for reasons of novelty and money-making, rather than equality and empowerment. Tattoo conventions, therefore, can be seen as problematic for several reasons. Women-only conventions are not as inclusive as they perhaps should be – they themselves risk excluding artists who identify as non-binary, for example, but who still require a safer-space alternative from the hyper-masculine environment of the traditional convention. Perhaps, therefore, what we are calling for is the assurance that *all* conventions are more inclusive, that they are safe and supportive environments for both artists and visitors of all genders – and that organisers ensure a diverse and inclusive judging panel.

Resistance Through Thought

As some participants expressed their resistance through action, others appeared to be re-thinking and re-conceptualising what tattoo has the potential to mean, to do and be. Tattoo in the interviews was discussed in terms of both a political act and a spiritual act, and both approaches were discussed in relation to what they could offer to the client – both specifically centring on women. LC's political stance identified a feminist consciousness, whereas IK's more spiritual approach was a

---

[3]Subsequent shows were different in that children were allowed to attend (although entertainment was still, as the interview illustrates, 'dancing girls and pin ups').

way of focusing on women clients through a therapeutic lens, more than a political one.

Previous research on women and tattooing considers tattooing as both a political act (Pitts, 1998) and a spiritual act (Pitts, 2003). Motives behind getting tattooed can certainly be analysed through a feminist lens, and much of the research discusses tattooing via feminist discourses such as reclaiming the body and empowerment (Atkinson, 2002; Dann, 2021; Pitts, 2003). What has not been addressed, however, is the process, practice and the role of the tattooer. If becoming tattooed can be considered a political act, then perhaps the act of making the tattoo could also be considered a political act. For women who become tattooed to reclaim their bodies, subvert mainstream gender norms or even more overtly, carry political messages, they (most often) rely on a tattoo artist to create the tattoo, enabling this reclaiming and subversion. These strategies for feminist, political or spiritual cultural production should, therefore, be explored as such.

> I feel lucky as a feminist to get to witness and aid women in claiming their bodies for their own. Most of my clients are women, and a number of them get tattoos despite what their parents or boyfriends want for them. I feel honoured to be part of women taking care of and taking control of their own bodies and at my best I can aid women in doing this, and not repeat experiences that disempower and subjugate them.
>
> LC

LC self-identified as a feminist in their interview, and it was evident that being a feminist was an important part of their identity, and something that influenced their practice as a tattooer. LC illustrates in the quote above how tattooing can be a feminist practice or process, with women making decisions about their own bodies despite the opinions of other people. The tattoo itself does not have to be a feminist image for the act of tattooing to have feminist intent.

LC also identifies the importance they attach to avoiding making clients feel uncomfortable and disempowered during the tattooing process. Several of the participants described the desire to reduce unequal power balances during the tattooing process, which is another example of the emotional labour employed by artists. This, I think, is comparable to the time and attention given to reducing the unequal power relations between the researcher and participants in feminist research. The similarities between the emotion work devoted to the breaking down of these boundaries suggest that artists like LC are engaging a level of feminist consciousness throughout and within their role and practices as a tattooer.

For the majority of the women I interviewed, the process of tattooing and ensuring a comfortable, equal, non-intimidating environment for their clients (regardless of gender) was as important as the end product, and this reflects what Amy Mullin (2003) describes in her paper on feminist art and political imagination. Mullin suggests that activist art and artists place equal care and importance on both the process of making the art and the final product, often seeing the process itself as part of this product (Mullin, 2003:203). Mullin also notes that feminist cultural production is often dismissed, and rarely considered 'art', due to 'misguided theories about the nature of art and the nature of politics' (Mullin, 2003:189). According to Mullin, 'good activist art works' do not need to convey a political message or propaganda; they may instead attempt to initiate dialogue or explore political alternatives (Mullin, 2003:195). Mullin is not discussing tattooing here, but this argument could helpfully be applied to the process of tattooing in some contexts; indeed, I discovered that although my research does not focus upon tattoo as art per se, I could draw upon work on feminist art to draw comparisons when considering tattoo as a political act and art in both form and practice.

Not all of the artists I interviewed identified as feminist, or even discussed feminism during their interviews, and, therefore, it is important to note that I am not arguing that women tattooing women is inherently feminist in theory or practice. Throughout IK's interview, her narratives and opinions appeared to embody a feminist consciousness and I did, therefore, ask directly about the potential link between feminism and her work as a tattooer. IK does not identify as feminist, although she did reflect on how her work might be perceived as 'feminist' in nature.

> Rather than women needing to make Feminist spaces in terms of place, I just think, for me, making intense work that is political or challenging, or in typically 'masculine' mediums (such as painting) is how I want to push the public. If I achieve that aim, then women will feel supported, included and spoken to, simply as a by-product.
>
> IK

What IK says here is in slight contradiction to what LC has expressed – rather than making safe, empowering spaces in order to challenge the dominant norms, IK talks about the art itself challenging these norms. Although IK is not presenting her work as feminist, there is an element of her work that politicises and challenges masculinity.

Asa Backstrom (2013), in her research on women in skateboarding, also notes that her participants rarely used the word *feminism* to describe themselves, but they used feminism as an influence and guide in 'doing' skateboarding culture differently (Backstrom, 2013:43) – just as IK seems to be using feminism as an influence in 'doing' tattooing differently. IK works from home and so, like LC, avoids the sexism and hyper-masculine studios prevalent in tattoo culture and is aware of their need to push boundaries and make a political statement. IK created and founded an all-women tattoo project, which she spoke about in her interview:

> I am currently working on a project that also happens to only include women that revolves around tattooing. I am working on what I call Spiritualist Tattooing, which involves the design of

abstract symbols and patterns for women to have tattooed as identifying markers which say something about their history, their life and what they would like to represent them. The tattoos themselves will be situated only on the stomach/torso, breasts, neck, face or head, as these are key powerful areas for women to receive a tattoo. I am inspired in this project by Oceanic cultures, where in times gone by, only women were tattooists and only women were tattooed- I am very interested in the fact that in some places it was an activity only for women, in opposition to our generally macho view of it. So I want to bring some of this idea of ritual to my practice, and for the tattoos to hold a kind of strength for the women who get them, understanding that tradition.

Perhaps the tattoos' meaning will be a secret only between ourselves, but I think that's a beautiful idea...the women who receive these tattoos will know they are a part of a larger project, but I don't want to fall into this idea of it being a 'brand', for want of a better word. It is simply the concept of women adorning themselves as a sign of strength and for a sense of belonging to something bigger than themselves that excites me about this.

So maybe I am a complete Feminist, I don't know, haha.

I am interested in making work which allows people whose voices are marginalised to take up some of the spotlight, so I think this is why I do so many projects which involve women, rather than starting with it as a 'cause'. Also, I don't feel as though I have a right to work toward giving men the same space, as I don't have an intimate knowledge of their life experience, so I feel that would be patronising of me.

IK

Here IK describes and explains the motivation behind her all-women project. 'Spiritualist tattooing' is a term she has developed to identify her tattoos and tattoo project as different from 'other' forms of tattooing; it illustrates how, in some ways, IK is thinking about tattooing differently from fellow artists. The areas of the body IK named as being a focus for the project are areas that up until recently have been quite unusual and somewhat taboo or stigmatised places for *anybody* to have tattooed, not only women – especially the face or head. Interestingly, this conflicts with what IK said in her interview about her own tattooed identity, and that she has avoided having publicly visible parts of her body tattooed. Previous research has addressed the placement of women's tattoos and suggests the placement of the image is central to tattoo projects that are motivated by cultural resistance (Atkinson, 2002: 229; Dann, 2021). By tattooing exposed or exposable areas of the body, such as arms, hands, lower legs and necks, women consciously engage in breaching established norms of femininity (Atkinson, 2002:229), and this is something embraced by IK's project.

IK also talks about the *ritual* of the tattooing, and this indicates that the process is as important (if not more so) than the tattoo itself. This, as discussed previously, relates to Mullin's work on feminist art and the focus upon process over product. IK does not identify as a feminist, nor does she equate the project with having feminist intention. IK states that the project is woman-focused without it centring on a 'cause' – so although IK does not see the project as feminist per se, it places women at the core without being explicitly political about that. However, IK is not opposed to using her art for political reasons as she states her work can be political and challenging. This perhaps mirrors the bigger issue of the complex relation between self-identification and the labelling of acts as *feminist*. Although certain acts, actions and ethos seem feminist to some, others may resist labelling them as such, which sometimes results in a disidentification with feminist consciousness (Scharff, 2010). This is illustrated in some ways by IK above. When she says, 'So maybe I am a complete Feminist, I don't know', she queries her own self-identification and alludes to perhaps not being sure whether she is a feminist, or not.

Tattoos for Survivors

As I was carrying out my fieldwork, there was an increase in media articles focusing on tattooists who were offering tattoos to survivors of domestic and sexual abuse. These artists included both women and men artists and illustrates how emotional labour has infiltrated some parts of the industry consciousness to influence the use of tattoo for more than decoration or aesthetics. As discussed in Chapter 2, the reclaiming properties of tattoo have been researched extensively (Craighead, 2011; Kosut, 2000; Pitts, 1998, 2003), but this previous research predominantly focuses upon the perspective of the individual survivor rather than the artist who is offering survivor tattoos as a 'service'. The media articles describe tattooists as 'healers' and 'therapists' (Mifflin, 2014) and highlight projects such as *Survivors Ink* – a project tattooing survivors of trafficking, abuse and addiction who were previously tattooed as a stamp of ownership by 'pimps' and raising funds for those women to have their tattoos covered up (Kelly, 2014). Articles such as these not only allude to the shift in how tattooing is utilised, but wide coverage of these projects and artists mean that non-tattooed members of the public are being presented with an alternative perspective on tattooing.

Tattoos for breast cancer survivors have also become increasingly prevalent and show an interesting intersection between medicine and subculture – some medical professionals offer medical tattooing on the breasts of women who have undergone mastectomies and reconstructive surgery, to imitate the nipples they lost through surgery. These tattoos lacked a degree of realism however, and soon tattoo artists were offering the same service, but with a wider range of ink shades than were available to surgeons and doctors, they could replicate a more realistic nipple. Similar to tattoos for survivors of abuse, this approach to tattooing illustrates how tattooing is being considered as something other than the aesthetic adorning of the body and the subverting rebellion of a subculture.

ML is a tattoo artist offering nipple tattoos to survivors and is somebody I interviewed via email about her work, having learned of her project via Twitter. ML founded a charity that raises funds for breast cancer survivors in the United States who need support with funding for medical treatment, reconstructive surgery and/or post-surgery tattooing.

> I got cold called in early 2011 from a cancer survivor who had been able to retain her natural breast on one side but had a mastectomy on the other side and then gotten a single implant. They offered a medical version of nipple tattooing at their offices but the patient was looking for something different. The medical version tended to be very flat and simple in nature, and she had seen a tattoo artist who was doing some incredibly realistic 3D nipple/areola tattooing for post mastectomy breast reconstruction.
>
> She wanted to see if she could find a woman tattooer to do it, and also stay close to home instead of having to drive 3 hours to have it done. She had been doing her own research and been calling multiple shops around the area up to the day she called me. When she asked if I thought I was interested and capable of what she wanted: a realistic looking 3D tattoo to match her natural nipple/areola on the other side - I said Yes without missing a beat.
>
> ML

When I re-interviewed KB in the second phase of interviewing, she too had started offering tattooing as a service for cancer survivors.

> I tattoo a lot of people who have been through really traumatic experiences, and coming to get their nipples tattooed can bring back so much stuff – they have to lie on a medical-looking bed, exposed, again, it can be re-traumatising. It's really difficult to know how to deal with that. I can't put myself in their shoes as I've never been through it. I feel very strongly about giving them the best I can give them – they have already been through so much. Often survivors are not happy with the medical grade tattoos they get after reconstruction – it's very different from getting a realistic nipple tattoo by an actual tattooer, and so I feel a sense of duty to make things better for them. I'm not saying that the medical grade tattoos are bad, it's just that they use different inks to us, and they fade, which means the empowerment fades with them. They have to go back for a yearly top-up, for someone who's been through

breast cancer, they don't want to have to go back to a hospital every year for that.

KB

Here KB demonstrates the emotional labour in tattooing cancer survivors and her strong desire and passion to do a good job for her customers. Not only does she want to ensure she tattoos well, but she is incredibly aware of her customers' own emotions and potential trauma – and puts things in place to help manage this.

> I've always had a separate room for the nipple tattooing – it's pink, girl, cute and nice with plants everywhere. I changed the name of my tattoo studio last year too, I know that some people aren't comfortable coming to a tattoo shop if they are coming to get areola tattoos, and so I removed the word tattoo from the name.
>
> KB

KB spoke about how many survivors are not tattooed anywhere else on their body, and are often people who wouldn't ever get tattooed in the traditional sense. And yet, due to invasive, life-changing surgery, are now in a position whereby they are relying on tattooing to re-gain a sense of self and empowerment. Changing the name of her studio seems like a drastic measure to ensure people are comfortable, but it shows the level of commitment and empathy held by KB in her work. We also see a focus on creating a calming and pleasant space in which to create the tattoo – echoing discussions above surrounding the importance of a safe space and what an impact this can have on customers.

Resistance Through Activism: #TattooMeToo

Throughout this book, I have discussed and highlighted the systemic, ingrained issues surrounding hegemonic masculinity that, until now, have been largely ignored or explained away as a normalised aspect of the sub-culture. The industry has been enabling sexist, misogynist behaviour, and for a long time, abusive artists have been very much 'hiding in plain sight' (Boyle, 2019:78). When then, stories began to surface of (some) male tattoo artists perpetrating sexual abuse, assault and harassment towards their clients, although these stories were horrific and upsetting – it really wasn't any surprise that this was happening in an industry that has harboured a harmful, sexist culture for decades.

> ...when you start looking back at stuff, and you think, actually, there's a few times when I should have said something [about inappropriate behaviour] and I didn't... and so I'm almost guilty by not pulling people up on stuff...we would often just pass stuff off as funny, but looking back, it needed challenging...
>
> KB

Male artists' attitude and treatment of women was part of the culture, seen as part of the risqué, dark side of tattooing, something that women just had to 'put up with'. However, as rape culture began to be called out and questioned in wider society, tattoo culture started to do the same. Rape culture is not a case of a 'few bad men' – it *is* a culture, enabled and perpetuated by society (Wilz, 2019:106) – and as the voices in this book show, perpetuated and to some extent enabled, by the tattoo industry and community also. I must note here that the artists I spoke to only ever referred to men artists as the perpetrators and women as the survivors of abuse, and so this is why I have discussed it in such binary terms here. I am in no way denying or dismissing that clients who identify as men may have also experienced abuse from tattoo artists, and this would make another important addition to scholarly work on the intersectional inequalities faced within the industry and community.

In October 2017, after numerous allegations of sexual harassment and assault against Hollywood movie producer Harvey Weinstein, the hashtag '#MeToo' dominated social media. Actor Alyssa Milano had taken to Twitter and encouraged women who had also been sexually harassed or assaulted by a man to tweet using #MeToo, in order to highlight just how prolific the problem was (Fileborn and Loney-Howes, 2019:3). In the first 24 hours of the hashtag being introduced, it had been used 12 million times. Similar movements began to surface – #timesup being one of them, driven by Hollywood actresses aiming to address the systemic problems with sexual harassment and assault in the workplace (Fileborn and Loney-Howes, 2019:4). These movements, much like the Black Lives Matter movement, soon trickled down into smaller industries, including the tattoo industry – who were soon to have their very own #MeToo moment.

UK-based tattoo artist Alex Bage started to speak out against abusive male artists in 2018 (Berg Olsen, 2018), after hearing numerous accounts and experiences of women being harassed, abused and taken advantage of by male artists. He began by speaking out on his Instagram page, posting the voices of the women who had shared their experiences with him. Bage was angered at men within the industry taken advantage of their power and status, and wanted to use his voice to raise awareness of the issues many tattoo clients were facing. Bage is a good example of how men within the industry *can* use their capital and associated power for good, assisting women in challenging the problematic and toxic behaviours of their colleagues. The #tattoometoo hashtag gained more traction in 2020 after hundreds of women took to Instagram to share their experiences of sexual abuse perpetrated by a number of prominent male tattoo artists. Tattoo magazine *Things and Ink* published an article focusing on how the industry was no longer a 'boys club' (Snape, 2020), and public discussion around sexual misconduct in the tattoo industry started to grow.

> . . .the only way I knew my abuser had abused other women, was via Instagram.
>
> anon

Whereas Twitter was the preferred platform for the #MeToo movement, Instagram was integral in tattoo's campaigning and was fundamental in #tattoometoo gaining so much traction so quickly. In Chapter 2, I discussed how Instagram has changed the world of tattooing significantly in terms of styles, trends and scenes within the community (Force, 2022) and we see here how important Instagram is for not only building an artists' brand, but for sharing knowledge and information also. Using Instagram meant that survivors could send their experiences to the account holder, and their voices could be posted anonymously. Names of abusive artists were called out, and comments under the posts started to piece together just how endemic the problem was. The same names were repeated, by different women – building a picture of not only the artist and abuser, but highlighting that the survivors were not alone in their experiences. The use of Instagram to do this also means that in terms of the abusive artist being called out so publicly, on a platform that is so integral to building a fan or client-base, this kind of negative publicity is particularly impactful and potentially damaging.

Although critics of the hashtag #MeToo have argued that it was useless, and unable to make a difference, campaigners and feminist scholars disagree, arguing that the movement has enabled a communal understanding of systematic rape culture (Wilz, 2019:137). It breaks the silence, raises awareness and develops a consciousness around sexual assault and rape, challenging norms and entrenched myths around sexual violence and giving survivors the opportunity to tell their stories in their own voices (Wilz, 2019:137–8). It also acknowledges that women's experiences are not isolated, but shared by others (Boyle, 2019:12).

> . . .if there's people commenting on this [abusive male tattooists], how many other people are there that are still being silent about it?. . . I started to kind of put feelers out and got in contact with other women who had similar stories and they got in contact with their friends who had had similar things. . . and I was like, there's a real need for a place where people can go and talk about this kind of thing and not feel like they're isolated or alone. A lot of the women that came forward had the same kind of questions – yeah so this has happened to me, but what now? What do I do about this? So there was a real need for basic education around what to do next if you have suffered any kind of abuse.
>
> TL

TSASS (@tsass_uk) – Tattoo Sexual Assault Survivor Support – was set up via Instagram as a page to raise awareness of sexual abuse and assault in the tattoo and piercing industry. It enables discussion around what is going on in the industry and community and allows survivors to share experiences and to get support.

> Initially I set up TSASS as a sort of 'let's talk about this' kind of page but I ended up getting hundreds and hundreds of different

messages and was like, wow, I'm really not equipped at the moment to be able to deal with the stuff that's coming in. So that led to me doing a mini-qualification with survivors of sexual abuse.

TSASS

The extent of the problem within the tattoo industry soon became apparent, and collectives such as TSASS started to work hard to provide support and advice for survivors. If we accept that cultural sexism exists (Savigny, 2021:24), then we can certainly acknowledge that sub-cultural sexism exists, and is a huge problem needing not only acknowledging, but addressing. The sexism and misogyny have been so normalised in both wider society and the sub-culture, that women have been 'disciplined into silence' for far too long (Savigny, 2021:19).

This silence is further perpetuated by the vastly unequal power dynamics within the tattoo industry, and it is important that we acknowledge the unique position of tattooers in terms of how they can use and abuse this power. If tattooists want to tattoo clients alone, they can very easily engineer this. It is easy to isolate a client – whether by ensuring no other artist is in the studio, or simply by closing the door to the room or drawing the curtain or screen. We must also consider the physicality of being tattooed – clients may be partially dressed, depending on what part of the body is being tattooed; they may be sat or laying in an awkward or potentially vulnerable position, and very often in pain. The tattoo artist is in a position of power throughout the appointment with access to the client's body – consensual access – meaning that the artist can often excuse or explain any 'accidental' touching as a mistake.

So what starts of as a sexual joke, that isn't necessarily crossing a line, they start off by testing the waters and then might move to a flirty comment, which might lead to inappropriate touching, so it's all about pushing a bit further each time but there's no firm boundary at the beginning to shut that down, there's no rule there.

TL

I would be interested to find out if there is a higher proportion of abusers in tattooing versus the general population or other industries... in the beginning, I didn't know what the motivation was behind sexual abuse... I didn't understand the motivation behind why people would perpetrate those kinds of offences... but having looked into it and once you understand that it's about power and control and you need to come with a sense of entitlement to be able to do that to somebody else, you can understand how the job would appeal to somebody that was like that or how they would abuse that position.

TL

As I have discussed in previous chapters, tattoo artists have a huge responsibility towards their clients – not only are they placing permanent ink on their bodies, but they are working very closely with and on the client's body. Anyone new to tattooing relies on the knowledge of the artist to guide them through the process and tattooers will 'educate and socialise them into a client-role while working to ensure the tattoo is accomplished as smoothly as possible' (Kiskaddon, 2021:307). This not only means that abusive artists can manipulate clients who are unfamiliar with the tattooing process, but it also has a significant impact upon the client's ability to challenge inappropriate behaviour by the artist.

In 2018, the hashtag #whyIdidntreport went viral on Twitter, with Twitter users sharing their personal experiences and reasons for not reporting sexual violence (Reich et al., 2022:470). Researchers examining the tweets found that the most frequent reasons for not reporting included the relationship to the perpetrator, self-blame, feelings hopelessness/helplessness, not expecting to be believed, minimisation and repression of the trauma and regret for not reporting (Reich et al., 2022:470). If we apply this to the world of tattooing, with the studio being the site of the abuse and the artist being the perpetrator, we can begin to unpack the complex circumstance of #tattoometoo survivors. Western society culturally and socially conditions us into thinking about rape and assault in very specific ways – stranger rape, for example, is something we are warned of, given advice around, usually with a focus on 'how to stay safe'. Because of these prevalent rape myths and stereotypes, many survivors don't think that their own experiences (of anything other than stranger rape) are 'bad enough' to warrant being labelled rape or sexual assault (Wilz, 2019:76). In the context of tattooing, survivors of abusive tattoo artists have chosen to be in the studio, have chosen this artist to tattoo them, they have consented to the tattoo on their body – and so when the artist is abusive towards them, it is difficult to make sense of what has happened. Many survivors will blame themselves, and many will even question whether their experience was abuse. Many survivors don't or didn't speak out – thinking they were alone in their experiences or were frightened of the consequences of calling out a well-known artist in a tight-knit community.

#Tattoometoo survivors also, like all survivors of sexual violence, have cultural norms and expectations of 'the perfect victim' to negotiate. The stereotype of the 'perfect' victim means that women are more likely to be believed if they are very young or very old, if they were assaulted by a stranger, if they suffer physical injury, if they are from the dominant ethic group in the society (and the perpetrator is not), if they are deemed 'sexually respectable', if they haven't been drinking or taking drugs and if they report the crime to the police immediately (Boyle, 2019:80). Women's credibility is under constant scrutiny (Boyle, 2019:80) – women who accuse or disclose sexual violence are doubted, questioned and asked to prove what they are saying is true. Add to this, the age-old stereotype of the tattooed woman being promiscuous and/or 'liking pain' or being somewhat sexually 'adventurous' (Swami and Furnham, 2007), tattooed women – especially heavily tattooed women – do not meet society's entrenched vision of the 'perfect victim' and

102 Tattooing and the Gender Turn

this, therefore, merely adds to the barrier to reporting or challenging abusive behaviour.

> ...it's a common thing, especially in tattooing, that these people [abusers] are probably quite talented artists, but that doesn't mean that what they did is somehow justified because they're good at what they do... a lot of people hide behind that I think that's disgusting.
>
> TL

As we have seen in previous chapters, sub-cultural capital is a powerful phenomenon, and many artists hold a lot of respect in the industry because of it. Not only, therefore, are survivors grappling with the idea that people outside of the tattoo community might not believe them if they speak out, but they must also consider whether people inside the community will believe them – or support the artist instead. To speak out about behaviour by somebody who is potentially liked and respected, in a community that is at times quite insular and self-policing, is a scary prospect. It also means speaking out against parts of a sub-culture one may have invested time and emotion in – with this investment comes a certain level of loyalty, which makes it difficult to criticise. Sara Ahmed's (2010) depiction of the feminist killjoy is useful here, being disappointed in something that is supposed to make us happy, or perhaps *used* to make us happy – not only means we experience a negative effect, but also places us 'at odds' with powerful (sub)-cultural norms (Boyle, 2019:94).

As the quote from TL above highlights, many artists hide behind their talent – 'good artists' are often excused for their behaviour in the industry, going unchallenged or accusations are ignored because of who the artist is. Society often awards straight white men with more credibility and authority simply because they are members of the dominant group, leading to a 'credibility gap' (Wilz, 2019:102) between male abusers and women survivors, and this is further perpetuated within tattoo culture, with the addition of sub-cultural capital.

For women speaking out about tattoo artists, 'discrediting' an artist who relies on tattooing to make a living is also a concern – the guilt of 'ruining' somebody's career is an additional barrier for survivors to face. Sympathy for the accused (Wilz, 2019:105) is something all survivors must negotiate, and this is a particular issue within the tattoo community – the thought of somebody losing their livelihood is a burden many survivors worry about. The impact of sexual violence upon the survivor is immense, and yet there is so often a quick shift in narrative and leads to men being framed as the effected party (Wilz, 2019:104). So what benefits, if any, does using social media for campaigns such as #tattoometoo offer survivors, and what impact does this have upon women speaking out against abusive artists? Do social media platforms offer a safe(r) space for survivors to call their abusers out?

The #tattoometoo movement was different from the movement within the film and media industry as it called out the abusers and allowed the survivors to be anonymous if they wished to be. Instagram accounts were set up to enable the account holder to share the experiences of others' anonymously. This put more of an emphasis on the accused, rather than the accuser. It served to centre men as the offenders and not the women as the victim or survivor – shifting and reframing the narrative from 'these are the women accusing' to 'these are the men being accused'. The posts also served as a warning to potential future clients of these artists, *therefore serving as a protective act as well as an act of resistance and defiance.* As Boyle (2019) argues, sharing experiences of men's violence against women cannot only be about telling women's stories; this risks making men's violence exclusively a women's issue and takes men out of the picture (2019:13). We need to ensure that men and the culture that enables their behaviour are very much framed as the issue here. Re-framing the narrative – making something visible that was once invisible – can shift the focus and highlight the problem (Boyle, 2019:25). In relation to the tattoo sub-culture, this could be applied to the 'banter' that we, who are familiar with male-dominated tattoo spaces, are all too accustomed to. For years, women have endured this (often) sexualised banter, without question or challenge, because it is framed as harmless 'fun', and is easy to brush off as such even if it is questioned. However, if we re-frame this, and call it harassment, it takes on a new meaning and we start to see it from the point of view of the woman, who may well have felt uncomfortable having to listen to this 'banter'. Women perpetually don't speak up for fear of not being believed, or fear of being blamed, or shamed, but the power behind women speaking up has the power to change the landscape of sexual violence (Savigny, 2021:17). Social media is being used as a tool to unite and gather stories – a site for speaking out safely, voices are being heard and activists can use it to connect, organise and protest (Savigny, 2021:20).

There are of course limitations to digital feminist movements – it relies on access to the internet and to these specific platforms, and on digital literacy. We also need to acknowledge that disclosures are not made without the risk of backlash – women especially are victims of online abuse, trolling and policing (Boyle, 2019:7), making it difficult and risky to disclose one's experiences, and even more difficult to name one's abuser (Boyle, 2019:11). Some feminists are critical of 'hashtag feminism' because it risks focusing on individual stories rather than changing bigger systems (Wilz, 2019:139) – but can the voicing of individual experiences lead to bigger change? Certainly, in the tattoo sub-culture, listening to and airing individual experiences is leading to a bigger, more structural shift – not only in the way sexual violence is acknowledged and considered, but in the action and activism needed to implement change within the industry.

Research by Kaitlynn Mendes and Jessica Ringrose (2019) identified #MeToo as a 'breaking point' for some of their participants who had shared their experiences by using the hashtag. Likening it to Sara Ahmed's 'feminist snap' – Mendes and Ringrose suggest it goes beyond individual empowerment, recognising that nothing would be done or would change without collective action (Mendes and Ringrose, 2019:40). Often, seeing other survivors voice their experiences gives other survivors the confidence to speak out, which, in turn, shifts the focus to the structural misogyny at play. In a sub-culture that has normalised misogyny for so long, women having their experiences finally heard by other members of the tattoo community was vital in their recovery. The internet and social media, therefore, may offer the 'potential or opportunity to build feminist communities across social, cultural, and global boundaries, and create feminisms that are nuanced, representative, and effective in establishing political and cultural change' (Rivers, 2017:127). Digital media is not perfect by any means – it may not be the complete utopian solution we wish for – however, digital media does hold potential for 'shouting back' (Turley and Fisher, 2018:131), and instigating the activism and resistance we so need.

Talking Action: Taking Action

The artists doing the resistance work in the industry, protesting against abusive men, supporting survivors and calling the abusers out are holding a lot of weight and responsibility. There is nothing else to stop these abusive men remaining in their role as tattooer, other than the community around them making it difficult or impossible for them to continue.

> ...the fact that tattooing is in its own little bubble, away from the rest of society and you're not held to the same standards.
>
> TL

Tattoo studios must adhere to local authority rules and regulations around hygiene and waste disposal, for example, but there is no legislation around the safety of clients in terms of the behaviour of the artist. Whilst other industries improve their processes in dealing with sex discrimination via formal and legal regulation, the same cannot be said of the tattoo profession (Thompson, 2015:124).

There are artists, accused of abuse during the #tattoometoo movement, who are still working as tattooists. They have been, and are being, excused of their behaviour, by other people in the industry and sub-culture. Men within the sub-culture are protected, not by legislation but *lack* of legislation and people within the community who are either ignoring their behaviour or excusing it. Deeply engrained sub-cultural sexism, coupled with long-standing sub-cultural capital and hierarchical relationships, means that certain men are allowed to get away with abusive, toxic behaviour. These men are made powerful from within the industry and community and are protected by the same structures. The tattoo industry, and community to some extent, has normalised sexist behaviour for a very long time – and only now are we seeing any kind of action against this. If we view the campaigning against sexual violence to be a turning point, then we need to think about the ways in which we (sub) culturally normalise sexism (Savigny, 2021:30). Social media has given women a platform to voice their experiences and be heard. But it is only the voices that are listened to that go on to create and form the catalyst for challenge and change. People will still make up their own minds about the perpetrator – there will be people who still book appointments with these abusive artists.

There are some very good men who are helping out with this. But unfortunately, it is a fact that the majority of this kind of abuse is being perpetrated by men and that makes a lot of men uncomfortable when you say that... and this you can understand when you see how society perceives men and excuses their behaviour. It's seen as a women's issue but it's an everyone issue, we all need to pulling our weight... there needs to be more work done by people who aren't survivors – it shouldn't just be on women and the survivors, survivors are already exhausted with battling through this every single day, the load needs to be shared more on men's side... it's unfortunate that it's men who are listened to more when they speak about this problem, that's what comes with male privilege, and the people in power also – it needs to be coming from them; I've heard very little from studio owners speaking up and saying, this is what we're doing to combat this problem.

TL

TSASS are calling for studios and studio owners/managers to act in improving their practises for the benefit of all clients. They have called for background checks on all artists – and have suggested that all artists should be Disclosure and Barring Service (DBS) checked before they start working in a studio. They ask for artists never to be working alone in the studio (suggesting a minimum of two artists at any one time); that studios should have a mission statement – outlining their stance on abuse in the industry and highlighting what they are doing to protect clients and colleagues. They also ask that studios take a zero-tolerance approach to certain behaviours. TSASS argue that these simple but effective actions should come from the top (studio owners) rather than survivors having to campaign to secure these changes. The capital that artists hold within the sub-culture could very easily be used to demand and ensure a safer environment for all members of the community – whether this capital is held by women or men artists.

There are resources out there that people can use as well – there's HR formats that people can use to combat sexual violence in the workplace that can be applied to any setting – and simple things, like making sure staff aren't left alone, or nobody tattoos outside of hours or an anonymous drop box where people can write about their experiences without naming themselves.

TL

Reminiscent of activism seen in the second and third wave of feminism, and taking on the DIY-activist ethos of the Riot Grrrl movement, there has been an increase in information around what is and is not acceptable behaviour in the tattoo studio. Using the tools of fourth wave feminism, these discussions usually take place via social media posts and make use of Instagram being an already well-used platform within the tattoo community. Along with @tsass_uk, Instagram accounts such as

@yourbody_yourtattoo have been created to make clients aware of their rights whilst being tattooed, with posts ranging from definitions of abuse and assault to what to do if you feel uncomfortable with your tattooist.

> I wanted to put together some little advice guides, on behaviour that is and isn't acceptable, or what ref flags to look out for, it's really difficult in a tattoo setting because yeah you can say that touching someone in an intimate place is not acceptable, but if they're doing that because you're having that area tattooed, there's a grey area, is that or isn't it appropriate touching for what's being done on that person and what the person has consented to.
>
> TL

By campaigning for change such as DBS checks in tattoo studios, and creating advice guides, women are paving the way for actual structural change to happen – building resistance against the sexism and misogyny, taking action to improve the industry and offering solutions to the problems.

> …as a survivor, you're already battling against the odds, you've already been put in a position of lesser than and made vulnerable by that abuser so to then try and speak out against them and almost squash them on to a lower level is really really difficult, but if you can do that from a position that's above that person, so maybe a studio owner that's cracking down on a staff member that's been accused of this kind of thing, it's a lot easier to come from the top down rather than the bottom up, which is what's needed.
>
> TSASS

We do have to acknowledge that it is predominantly women artists doing the *work* here, and that this work requires commitment and organisation (Boyle, 2019:26) – in addition to their day jobs as tattooers, they are voluntarily taking on extra labour to campaign, manage social media accounts, respond to messages from survivors and create content around supporting and advising not only survivors but all tattoo clients – some even completing specialist qualifications in order to better support survivors. The level of emotional labour employed by artists undertaking this work cannot be ignored – responding to disclosures of sexual abuse, or offering advice around abusive behaviour is tiring, traumatic and can lead to burn-out. The Instagram accounts that have been created specially to advise clients of their rights in the tattoo studio, and what to do if they feel vulnerable or unsafe, reduces the pressure somewhat from answering individual queries – although some artists are still responding to direct messages, feeling a sense of responsibility towards survivors. In this context, 'discursive activism' (Mendes, 2015) has the power and potential to make an impact on how the tattoo industry moves forward in its treatment of women and other vulnerable or minority groups, and women are working hard – both physically and emotionally – for this change.

Initiatives such as *Cover Ups Against Abuse* have collated and compiled lists of artists who are volunteering their time, artistry and skills to cover up the tattoos of abusive artists – free of charge – for survivors. Wearing the tattoo work of your abuser is a constant reminder of the experiences they put you through, and so being able to eradicate this from your skin, for many, is a powerful and empowering step towards recovery. Mirroring sentiments discussed above of artists covering work on survivors of domestic and sexual abuse, this once again, shows how artists – of all genders – are embracing emotional labour, whilst using their physical labour and capital, to reduce the emotional and physical trauma caused by abusive artists. This collective action is a powerful tool of resistance against the harmful sections of the sub-culture, and sends a message to the community that the industry is taking a stand.

We do also have to acknowledge the risk that artists are taking by engaging in campaigns against sexual abuse in the tattoo industry. All artists need to make a living, and although resistance is needed, it may impact upon their ability to make money. Backlash against feminist activism is always a risk, and when this activism is taking place in the tattoo sub-culture, the risk of backlash from the community may be amplified. Artists might, therefore, be actively risking their reputations and livelihoods to campaign and change the industry.

> This is the second time [we] have tried to push this petition [for DBS checks to be used in studios] through because in the beginning, lots of people were saying it was discriminating against those who have minor convictions or are reformed characters. Our intentions from the start weren't to worry about the low level things, but I feel that if you've murdered someone, or been sexually abusive, or harmed someone in some way, you shouldn't be tattooing the general public. We're not trying to ruin people's lives, but they shouldn't have access to people's bodies in such an intimate context.
>
> TSASS

There is somewhat of an intra-sub-cultural resistance happening, women are not colluding with the hyper-masculinity of the culture, but instead are creating women-only space and/or queer spaces which are open and welcoming to not only women but queer, non-binary, trans people and people of colour, as well as other vulnerable or minority groups – by successfully introducing a focus upon emotional labour, activism and a general sense of 'not putting up with this anymore', feelings of powerlessness amongst women and minority groups have the potential to finally be reversed.

Conclusion

These resistant acts and activist campaigns do not avoid challenges; however, women, non-binary and queer artists continue to intervene and disrupt the dominant structure, and in doing so they are challenging the hegemony, and creating micro-cultures of safe spaces for women and other minority groups. Tattooing, when considered in this context, could be deemed a mode of feminist cultural production. Artists are pushing the boundaries of what is and is not 'acceptable' within tattoo culture, and not only creating safe spaces which employ a feminist ethos but challenging and changing the way the industry structure is formed, maintained and reproduced.

Women, non-binary and queer artists are navigating the industry not only through tattooing, but through language, media, community and ways of thinking about tattooing. Many artists are centralising the experience of getting tattooed, placing the customer and the customer's experience at the forefront, and emotionalising the interaction. Women have been and continue to be influential in the resistant micro-cultures within the sub-culture, producing different knowledge which, in turn, challenges the dominant sub-cultural systems. If we consider gender as a discursive framework (Cohn, 1993), we can see how many tattoo artists are creating *new* discursive frameworks – producing, creating and maintaining safer spaces for those who are women, queer and people of colour.

Tattoo culture has had, and continues to have, a complex and nuanced relationship with ideologies in and around acts of resistance. Although, in many ways, becoming tattooed is no longer seen as an act of resistance, there remain resistant acts within tattoo culture. We can also see how these resistant acts are influenced by bigger movements within wider society. Just as the #MeToo movement was 'discursive activism' (Boyle, 2019:3) which aimed to change what sexual harassment and assault meant, by increasing awareness of who its victims and survivors were – #tattoometoo aimed to raise awareness of sexual misconduct happening in a sub-culture, by artists who hold capital, respect and are at the 'top of their game' – and that it was happening to hundreds of women. This broadens the understanding that harassment and assault is perpetrated not by the odd rogue man, but by lots of men who are liked and respected by hundreds of people in their industry. And that their victims and survivors are numerous and could be anyone. Speaking out may not be an end to violence, but it is the start of ending violence against women (Boyle, 2019:24). By hearing how frequent these acts of violence occur, and how normalised it has become in certain pockets of the industry, we can now recognise and acknowledge that this is a structural issue, not an individual one.

Chapter 6

Conclusion: Deconstructing Binaries, Exposing Paradoxes

Researching a culture that was once so familiar to me has revealed numerous contradictions and conflicts that I could not have predicted. As a researcher, this makes for a fascinating project; from a personal perspective, it leads me to reflect upon and question whether I really knew the culture at all. How can a sub-culture that seemingly promises freedom, community and autonomy create such profound feelings of restriction, exclusion and conformity?

What surprises, as well as disappoints, me is the similarities between the experiences of the women artists discussed in Chapter 1 – the women artists who paved the way for the artists of today – and the experiences of the artists I interviewed for this book, centuries later. Issues such as male gatekeepers, male bias and sexism were all documented by the first women artists of the nineteenth century and continue throughout the twentieth and twenty-first centuries. The interviews and subsequent discussions throughout each chapter of this book have exposed these similarities with historical experiences, but also unexpected paradoxes within the narratives themselves. I found in participants a sense of ambivalence towards how to navigate and negotiate those paradoxes, whilst attempting to manage relations within and outside of the industry. Conflicts between counterculture and the mainstream, resistance and conformity and dominant and alternative femininities were all central to my research, underpinned by various negotiations of capital and status, and complicated by the juxtaposition of sub-cultural leisure activities, labour and employment. By exploring the nuances of these complex negotiations, I have offered an insight into the gender relations within the tattoo industry.

Sub-cultural Paradoxes

Chapter 3 explored women's experiences of the tattoo industry. Many of the participants described a career in tattooing as offering an opportunity for freedom in the workplace to 'be themselves', and avoid the constraints associated with more mainstream occupations. However, as the interviews progressed, what appeared amongst the narratives of freedom and choice was a paradox between

Tattooing and the Gender Turn, 109–118
Copyright © 2023 Emma Beckett
Published under exclusive licence by Emerald Publishing Limited
doi:10.1108/978-1-80262-301-720231006

an individual sub-cultural career that promised a sense of personal independence and autonomy, and a hierarchical sub-cultural industry, structurally built around a hegemonic masculinity with a bias against women artists. This left many of the artists in a position whereby they were either compelled to conform to certain industry norms, or resist, with possible consequences. The very field offering freedom and choice to women who affiliate with an alternative femininity was also a field that constrained and restrained the same artists.

These constraints were further illustrated through the difficulty experienced when the participants tried to establish themselves within the industry. Male gatekeepers often chose men over women to take up apprenticeships, and the capital afforded to them meant that being a man in the industry often held an immediate position of status and authenticity when compared to women. The ability and opportunity to be 'themselves', therefore, was not an opportunity open to all women who attempted to enter the industry. Previously accumulated sub-cultural capital did appear to be useful in the transition from consumer of tattoos to producer. Women and queer artists who had participated in alternative subcultures and associated with countercultural lifestyles were able to use this capital to gain a 'foot in the door' – they may have known artists or studios and engaging with an alternative 'look' meant they held a degree of aesthetic capital also. However, the participants were aware of the existence of a hegemonic masculinity within the industry, and sometimes presented or acted as 'one of the boys' to fit in and succeed. Many of the women who described 'fitting in' with the dominant masculinity did not consider this a purposeful act, but rather described themselves as routinely identifying with certain aspects of 'masculine' behaviour (identifying as a 'tomboy', for example) and, therefore, being 'one of the boys' appeared to be easy for them.

This leads to another important paradox within the narratives. The structure of the sub-culture is one which, on the one hand, can free women from mainstream employment pressures and on the other hand, is dominated by hegemonic masculinities and male gatekeepers. It is also evident that once women have secured their space within the field, they are sometimes expected to adopt or appropriate the masculine nature of the field to remain and thrive in the industry. What the interviews also illustrated, however, was that many of the women, once they had secured their position in the field, were then able to, and actively did, use their 'femininity' to progress their work, their role and their economic capital by giving them a distinctive profile. This profile set them apart from men colleagues and generated a 'unique selling point'.

Not Too Feminine, but Feminine Enough

The participants, many of whom had been engaging with alternative subcultures since their teens, displayed their alternative femininities through dress, lifestyle and now occupation. They had actively resisted mainstream notions of femininity, dyeing their hair, becoming tattooed and/or pierced, and had actively sought a non-mainstream career historically framed as a 'man's job'. However, during the interviews, many of the women talked about utilising their femininity in their role as tattooists. Traits associated with being feminine, such as caring, listening, being attentive, were all aspects of tattooing that the participants said they paid particular attention to for the benefit of their clients and for their own professional fulfilment, and many felt this was an imperative part of their career as a tattooist. And so, the women who had actively resisted, avoided and subverted mainstream notions of femininity, and very often performed or displayed alternative femininities in terms of aesthetics, were now using the qualities very much associated with dominant versions of femininity to offer a better service to their clients, thus highlighting the ambivalences involved in performing and displaying femininities.

The participants described being able to offer a different kind of service than their male colleagues, focusing strongly (though not exclusively) upon the typically feminine traits already identified. Men can, of course, adopt these supposed feminine traits, but women artists are using traits typically associated with being a woman to stand out from the hegemonic masculinities, not only offering a different service to what many of the men artists can offer but, in turn, increasing their economic capital when clients choose them over male artists. The discord arises, therefore, when we consider that the qualities the women are using to distance themselves from the hegemonic masculinity of the industry are the qualities associated with typically 'feminine' women, and, therefore, qualities that reinforce mainstream gender norms and stereotypes. The distinguishing factor associated with women artists both disrupts the gender order and simultaneously reinforces the stereotype many of the women strive to subvert.

It appears, therefore, that there are two elements of constraint at play for women in the industry. Firstly, on initial entry to the industry, being a woman can in some cases inhibit or hinder the transition from consumer to producer. Secondly, when working within the industry, women who utilise their 'femininity' risk reinforcing some of the gender stereotypes they were originally attempting to subvert. There is, thus, a nuanced negotiation to navigate – between being 'one of the boys', appropriating masculine capital for the sake of a place within the field, and utilising typically feminine traits to distinguish oneself from the hegemonic masculinity, and offer clients something different, without compromising the notion of 'alternative femininities', or reinforcing gender stereotypes.

The complexities of being a woman tattoo artist are evident throughout the narratives, but what my research also illustrates is that artists are attempting to disrupt these constrictions and obstructions, by *reclaiming constraints as an agentic act*. Indeed, for many of the women, it was important that they were making a purposeful difference to the experience they were offering their clients. There was a distinct focus on emotional labour as part of the body work experience and this became apparent as being equally important in the tattooing process as the tattoo itself. Although the presumption that women artists by nature are more caring and attentive than men artists risks reinforcing the essentialist notion that women are 'natural' care givers and men are not, focusing upon *feminine* capital, rather than *female*, means we can uncouple the two and explore the possibilities of all artists utilising this capital for the benefit of clients, further disrupting the very narrow hegemonic masculinity of the industry.

The uncoupling of feminine and female capital is more complex than this, however, and it is, therefore, important to unpack the nuances surrounding both forms of capital, and how they are utilised by men and women artists. In Chapter 4, I suggested that women are often not rewarded for displaying typically feminine qualities in the workplace due to an expectation on women to utilise these qualities 'naturally', unlike men who, with no expectation to uphold typically feminine qualities, do in turn, get rewarded. However, I also argued that this may differ for women who regularly display alternative femininities, because women who do not conform to mainstream notions of femininity are often deemed 'unfeminine' and, therefore, presumed 'lacking' in qualities associated with dominant versions of femininity. This, therefore, further illustrates the complex and often contradictory nature of femininity within the sub-culture. Women who do not always adhere to dominant norms of femininity, and, therefore, are not deemed typically feminine by those who value dominant gender norms, but display typically feminine traits (caring, listening, being attentive, for example), may experience rewards for this in terms of increase in clients, economic capital and positive client feedback. However, some aspects of femininity were also dismissed by artists – both women and men – and this led to the downplaying of elements considered too feminine, and too 'girly', such as the use of pink tattoo equipment. During the interviews, and as discussed in Chapter 3, overly-feminised equipment was identified as something to be avoided, in order to be taken seriously by fellow (men) artists. Being *visibly* overly-feminine appears to be criticised, and yet *invisible* femininity is not. This demonstrates the continuous flux and negotiation of femininity that women artists engage in, in order to manage their positions within the industry.

Holland's (2004) use of *flashing femininity* and my own discussion around a *masculine masquerade* can both be considered as a form of gendered emotional labour and as discussed above, women tattoo artists utilise both masculinised and feminised emotion work in order to succeed in the industry. I would argue, therefore, that perhaps the type of emotional labour displayed here is not *gendered labour* as such, but rather *gender labour* and relies upon the individual utilising specific gendered traits in order to succeed in their field. I argued in Chapter 4 that feminine traits, and therefore *feminine capital*, can be appropriated and utilised by men artists much like masculine capital was appropriated by some of the women I interviewed. However, the women also illustrated the presence of *female capital*, and this is something the men artists are unable to access. Female capital was useful capital when clients simply, for various reasons, wanted to be tattooed by a woman. There is no doubt that some tattoo clients – women, men and non-binary – will actively seek out and choose women artists over men, in the same way that patients opt for a woman GP, for example. This could illustrate a presumption (by the client/patient) regarding the emotional labour or the qualities a woman practitioner might offer, or it could mean that due to the body work involved in the transaction, the client simply feels more comfortable with the body worker *not being a cis man*. By navigating a space in the industry, therefore, women, non-binary and queer artists are providing services to those clients, of all genders, who, for whatever reason, do not want to be tattooed by a cis man. This is of benefit to both the artists and the clients and is an example of reclaiming the original constraint of *not being a male artist* and converting this into a capital-yielding and profitable agentic act. Artists can also utilise their *queer capital* (Kjaran and Jóhannesson, 2016) in the creation and maintaining of queer-friendly studios. Ensuring a safe space for not only clients but for artists, and through the space they nurture, women, non-binary and queer artists are challenging the hegemony of the masculine studio culture – which again can be seen as a profitable *and* agentic act of resistance.

'Selling Out' or Just Selling? Ambivalence and the Mainstream

Not only did the interviews show the complex dynamic between gendered capitals and hegemonic versions of gendered traits, they also exposed a nuanced relationship between sub-cultural capital and the mainstream. As discussed in Chapter 3, with tattooing becoming increasingly popular outside of sub-cultural aesthetics, tattoo artists are often granted levels of capital amongst mainstream culture. Because of this, I would argue that we could consider the tattoo sub-culture as a *mainstreamed sub-culture*. Throughout the narratives, there was a degree of ambivalence surrounding this capital – depending upon who held the capital, who awarded the capital and how the capital was utilised. Capital gained and maintained within the sub-culture was always useful, respected and appreciated by artists. This was not the case for capital held within the mainstream, which was not always useful and was sometimes disregarded or actively dismissed. The narratives illustrated how this ambivalence was centred around the *wrong or right* kind of capital.

The ambivalence derived from the fact that many of the artists felt fondly towards tattooing as a culture, and one that had until relatively recently been somewhat of a 'secretive' counterculture, existing on the peripheries of the mainstream. However, with the influence of television shows and the advertising industry, the celebritisation of tattooing and the general increase in interest in tattooing as an art form, the mainstream in many Western countries has begun to appropriate tattooing and see tattoo artists as individuals who hold status and capital. For many artists, this is problematic. There is, for some, a desire to keep tattooing as a sub-cultural art form and retain a distance from a mainstream culture which threatens to dilute the significance of the counter-cultural aspects of this sub-culture. However, this desire is matched with a want for tattooing to be taken seriously as an art form and to be legitimised and viable as a career choice and livelihood. Economic capital is important: tattoo artists must make money, and an increase in interest from the mainstream leads to an increase in clients, and a rise in economic capital for the artist. This leads to a sense of wanting to remain on the peripheries of the mainstream, and yet wanting also to utilise the mainstream's opportunity for seriousness and legitimacy, at the same time as not wanting to be considered as 'selling out' by one's peers. There is, however, a degree of unavoidable conformity that needs to be upheld if tattoo artists want to be successful in their field. Legal issues – including obtaining a council licence to open a studio and strict health and safety policies and procedures – are all vital in the professionalisation of the industry and central to the viability and success of the artist and the studio. And so, artists need to utilise mainstream structures to succeed and progress, and are because of this, in many ways, legitimised by these mainstream institutions, at the same time as striving to retain their sub-cultural status.

Kat Von D, although no longer in the spot-light as often as she used to be, is a good example of the paradox between 'selling out' and being successful outside of the sub-culture, and further illustrates the additional layer of negotiation required by many women artists in the industry. Women are frequently placed as the 'other' within the sub-culture, a sub-culture that is already negotiating its own status within the mainstream. Thus, women are left wanting to be taken seriously both inside and outside of the sub-culture. Kat Von D became somewhat of an embodiment of this conflict between the mainstream and counterculture, and the ambivalence felt by her fellow artists vis-à-vis mainstream success. She was criticised by some participants for 'selling out' to the mainstream and for using her femininity in a way that some of the participants felt uncomfortable with. However, she was also praised and respected by some participants for the positive influence she has had upon women artists, and for encouraging more women into the industry.

Many of the artists I interviewed also talked about wanting to, or feeling the need to, manage the 'image' of the tattoo artist, and attempting to influence the perception of tattoo artists held by people outside of the sub-culture. This not only illustrates the complex relationship between the *insider* and the *outsider* of the sub-culture but is another example of how the women *laboured* to manage impressions and relationships. Both emotional and aesthetic labour was described by many of the participants as a way of managing the paradoxical relationship between wanting to remain on the peripheries of mainstream culture, but also not wanting to appear *too* deviant. These discussions also identified a complex fluidity between aesthetic *capital* and aesthetic *labour*. What constituted aesthetic capital inside of the sub-culture (having extensive visible tattoo coverage, looking 'alternative', for example) did not always function as aesthetic capital outside of the sub-culture, in fact alternative aesthetics often operated as the antithesis to capital outside of the sub-culture. And so, aesthetic labour was required to enable the artists to manage their aesthetic capital successfully and create a balance between being taken seriously outside of the sub-culture, avoid being labelled as *too* deviant by outsiders but at the same time, be *deviant enough* to retain a degree of aesthetic capital (and subsequent professionalism) inside of the sub-culture.

Resistance Is Not Futile

Resistance is fluid and complex. As my research illustrates, some participants exercised their agency but were not necessarily displaying resistance. Likewise, conformity to hegemonic structures did not necessarily indicate a lack of agency; conformity was sometimes used as a vehicle for resistance. For instance, as discussed throughout the research, some participants were able to utilise elements of a hegemonic masculinity to gain space within the industry with intention to 'change' or 'improve' the culture from their position as an insider.

Resistance is further complicated when considered in the context of main-streamed sub-cultures and alternative femininities. To describe potential resistant action as either resistant *or* conforming creates a false binary and is, therefore, problematic. Saba Mahmood (2005), in her book *Politics of Piety: The Islamic Revival and the Feminist Subject*, argues that discussions surrounding agency and conformity, resistance and submission are more complex than these binaries suggest. She argues that agency can be present 'not only in those acts that resist the norms but also in multiple ways in which one inhabits norms' (Mahmood, 2005:15). It is important to note the complexities and problems of conflating resistance with agency, in relation to tattoo culture, and my research further illustrates the complex negotiations at play within the sub-culture. Firstly, conformity does not necessarily mean a lack of agency and it is important to question the dominant binary of agency versus conforming. Secondly, resistance within subcultures is the norm – as I discussed in chapter two, subcultures are historically associated with resistance and subverting mainstream norms – and so, to *resist* the mainstream from a position of subcultural or sub-cultural insider is, in fact, to *conform* to the norms of the sub-culture.

In Chapter 5, I discussed how, with tattooing shifting from being a counter-cultural practice to one embraced by numerous groups within the mainstream, becoming tattooed can no longer be considered as an entirely resistant act. However, as my research shows, there are elements of resistance within the tattoo culture – including the relationship between alternative femininities and dominant versions of femininity. As discussed previously, women displaying alternative femininities (and, therefore, seemingly resisting mainstream notions of what it is to be 'feminine') are embracing the more traditional notions of 'femininity', such as caring, listening and being attentive, as a way of resisting the hegemonic masculine norms of tattoo culture. This not only illustrates, as discussed above, the complex relationship between alternative and dominant versions of femininities but also the nuances of resistance. The participants resisted certain elements of the hegemony, at the same time, as they reproduced other elements of the sub-cultural hegemony and/or the broader social hegemony. Although I discussed above the problematic reinforcing of gendered norms through focusing on 'feminine qualities', I would argue that by resisting certain elements of gendered hegemony, such as subverting mainstream norms attached to the feminine body, the participants are also able to *disrupt* mainstream ideologies of femininity and masculinity. Resistance to gender norms, therefore, exists hand in hand with complicity with, and conformity to, these norms – illustrating that resistance is indeed, contextual and fluid (Haenfler, 2004:408).

The most notable inter-sub-cultural resistance to date, perhaps, is the work of the artists surrounding the #tattoometoo movement. As Chapter 5 highlighted, the artists involved in not only raising awareness of the widespread issue of sexual abuse in the industry but actively fighting it – campaigning for changes in attitudes and practice – these artists are going above and beyond their role as tattooers. Abusive artists are being called out, customers are being educated in what is and is not acceptable behaviour in the studio, advice is given around tattoo red flags and what to do if your artist behaves in an undesirable manner. Advice is also offered to studios in how to ensure clients are safe throughout the tattoo process, and efforts are being made to encourage policies and procedures are put in place as a formal arrangement to ensure client safety. Throughout this book, I have spoken about negotiation and compromise – and yet, what we see here, finally, is an unapologetic resistance against the problematic male domination of the sub-culture.

Conclusion: Tattooing and the Gender Turn

With a focus on gender, my research has highlighted important discussions surrounding subcultures, sub-cultures and the fluid movement between counterculture and the mainstream. I have explored the structural organisation of male-dominated subcultures and found the tattoo industry to be both emancipatory and constricting for many artists entering and continuing to work in the field. The conflicting nature of the industry led to nuances in how artists managed their position in the field, underpinned by complex negotiations of capital: both sub-cultural and gendered. I suggested that tattoo artists are *trans-sub-cultural practitioners*, who transcend various subcultures and sub-cultures, whilst working in a collective of artists that at times is subcultural-like in its structure and intra-relations. This is further complexified for women, non-binary and queer artists as they not only strive to be taken seriously in mainstream culture but the sub-culture also. This, as my research illustrates, can lead to resistance from minority artists.

The artists I spoke to were often resisting elements of both the mainstream and the sub-culture, meaning they were in a position of resisting the alternative space they had originally sought for safely resisting the mainstream. This led to contradictions and ambivalence. Along with this resistance, came a level of conformity to elements of both the mainstream and the sub-culture, and so there appeared to be a continuous flux of resistance and conformity between both the sub-culture and the mainstream, illustrating how fluid resistance and conformity are.

Not only does this research expose this fluidity between conformity and resistance but also between mainstream and counterculture, and dominant and alternative femininities. Throughout the book, I have problematised and deconstructed the binaries surrounding these three key areas, illustrating how they are not always binary in structure, and do not always exist in opposition to each other – in fact, in the context of my research they are rarely in opposition, but instead are fluid, contingent and context-specific. It is vital to unpack the normativity and the norm-creating expectations of a sub-culture or subculture. Are there really clear and concise boundaries between a 'mainstream' and 'subculture'? My research shows a fluidity and flux between sub-cultures and what might be deemed the mainstream; just as there is between resistance/submission and agency/conformity. Within subcultures (or sub-cultures), being resistant *is normative*. Therefore, in this context, enacting a resistance to the mainstream is expected by the sub-cultural norms, and is, in its own way, conforming. Some, but not all, women, non-binary and queer tattooers today are placing themselves at the centre of a resistant space – offering an alternative to what have become the norms of the sub-culture.

Tattoo research shows the relatively new phenomenon of clients sharing their life stories, life experiences and reasons for getting tattooed with their artists, and some (DeMello, 2000; Pitts, 2003; Thompson, 2015) have argued that this has been associated with a middle-class 'self-help' discourse within tattooing. This, then, could be further related to the 'tattooist as therapist' narrative discussed throughout this book. However, what the literature does not consider is that the 'self-help' narrative equated with the middle-classes could also be the result of the influence of more women artists in the industry. Have women helped to transform mainstream perceptions of tattoo culture? Conversation, sensitivity and being more emotionally aware are often seen as more feminine traits, and this has been overlooked in research on the changing nature of the industry. Why equate emotion work so readily with the middle-classes but not with the increase in both women artists in the industry and women clients in the community? Dominant masculinities and femininities have been problematised throughout my research, and women's narratives describing the uses and value of feminine and female capital illustrated how both can be utilised productively and positively to disrupt hegemonic versions of gender. Therefore, my research expands upon work by Ross-Smith and Huppatz (2010), exploring gender as a form of capital and appreciating both femaleness and femininity as forms of 'embodied cultural capital' (2010:549). This, in turn, supports the women artists in their agentic acts of resistance and conformity.

Previous research on tattoos and tattooing has focused upon women as consumers rather than producers, because historically more women have been customers than tattoo artists. However, with numbers of women tattoo artists increasing, literature and research is beginning to highlight this. Previous work has not fully addressed the intersection of tattooing as an industry or form of employment and gender relations within the field. Neither has existing literature fully explored what it means to be a cultural producer within a sub-cultural field which is rapidly being embraced and appropriated by mainstream culture. The tattoo industry, as my research illustrates, is still a predominantly masculine space, and yet, existing research has largely ignored gender in its exploration of tattooing as a changing field of production and employment and has failed to consider tattooing as a gendered sub-cultural space or acknowledge the negotiations navigated by women tattooers in relation to gender, capital, labour and resistance.

This research contributes to ongoing academic discussions surrounding alternative femininities and resistant acts, but also male-dominated subcultures and women's negotiation of their position within these cultures. Although the research is seemingly focused on a niche sub-cultural context, findings from my research could be applied to similar male-dominated spaces – both in subcultures and in employment or work cultures. My research offers insights into the negotiations of both dominant and alternative femininities in the workplace and/or male-dominated spaces and opens opportunities to continue these conversations.

I have identified a complex inter-dependent relationship between alternative cultures and the mainstream, intersected by complex notions of both sub-cultural and gendered capital, which is further complicated by the dependency on economic capital and ambivalent investment in professional success. Engaging in research and subsequent theorising around the negotiation of femininities can be useful in a wider context of male-dominated fields – both in subcultural and mainstream cultures. By engaging with alternative versions of gender and utilising multiple versions of capital, individuals and collectives can intervene, interrupt and disrupt the hegemonic masculinities so dominant and problematic within male-dominated cultures and fields, like tattooing.

Women, non-binary and queer tattoo artists embody the intersections and complex relations between subcultures, mainstream culture, gender, employment and different forms of labour: body, emotional and aesthetic. Without exploring these artists in the tattoo industry, it would be difficult, perhaps impossible, to see how these seemingly opposing spheres are so intrinsically interrelated. Women have had to and still are negotiating their femininities and challenging the boundaries of social acceptability at the same time as using tattoo as a vehicle for independence, whilst navigating a male-dominated, narrowly masculine culture. Women, non-binary and queer tattoo artists exist in a culture that prides itself on being resistant and yet whilst existing in the sub-culture, they are continuously managing sets of norms, differing versions of capital and negotiating conformity. The sub-culture, in many ways, offers a sense of liberation, freedom and choice for tattoo artists and yet in many ways, the daily lived experiences of women, non-binary and queer artists show sub-cultural constraints and dominant norms for them to resist.

Women engage in continuous negotiations surrounding gendered norms and often need to downplay their femininity in order to successfully manage their everyday experiences of the tattoo sub-culture. As I have also discussed, women utilise certain gendered traits for the benefit of both their client and themselves. Women and queer artists are found to be creating and producing a new language and framework of resistance, and, in turn, are beginning to create a new system of norms surrounding gender, alternative identities and sub-cultures. Drawing upon DeMello's (2000) suggestion that there is a 'middle-class turn' in tattooing, I suggest that tattooing has undergone a *gender turn* which has led to a significant shift in the gender relations within the tattoo sub-culture. This gender turn has seen an increase in women, non-binary and queer folk to the tattoo sub-culture (both in terms of customers and artists) and the emotional and aesthetic labour invested by many women, non-binary and queer artists means that the masculine culture, and image, of the industry has the potential to shift – making it a safer and more inclusive space for everyone.

Bibliography

Ackerly, B.A. and True, J. (2020). *Doing Feminist Research in Political and Social Science*. Bloomsbury Publishing Plc.

Adams, J. (2012). Cleaning up the Dirty Work: Professionalization and the Management of Stigma in the Cosmetic Surgery and Tattoo Industries. *Deviant Behavior*. 33(3), 149–167.

Ahmed, S. (2010). Killing Joy: Feminism and the History of Happiness. *Signs: Journal of Women in Culture and Society*. 35(3), 571–592. ISSN 0097-9740.

Al-Kadhi, A. (2017). The Queer Tattoo Artists Reviving the Craft's Rebel Roots: The Power of Ink on the Skin. *huckmagazine.com*. available: www.huckmagazine.com/art-and-culture/queer-tattoo-artists/ [accessed 03.03.2017].

Ashforth, B. and Kreiner, G. (1999). How Can You Do It? Dirty Work and the Challenge of Constructing a Positive Identity. *Academy of Management Review*. 24(3), 413–434.

Atencio, M. Beal, B. and Wilson, C. (2009). The Distinction of Risk: Urban Skateboarding, Street Habitus and the Construction of Hierarchical Gender Relations. *Qualitative Research in Sport and Exercise*. 1(1), 3–20.

Atencio, M. (2008). "Freaky Is Just How I Get Down": Investigating the Fluidity of Minority Ethnic Feminine Subjectivities in Dance. *Leisure Studies*. 27(3), 311–327.

Atkinson, M. (2002). Pretty in Ink: Conformity, Resistance, and Negotiation in Women's Tattooing. *Sex Roles*. 47(5/6), 219–235.

Atkinson, M. (2003). *Tattooed: The Sociogenesis of a Body Art*. University of Toronto Press.

Atkinson, M. (2004). Tattooing and Civilizing Processes: Body Modification as Self-Control. *Canadian Review of Sociology & Anthropology*. 41(2), 125–146.

Ambrosch, G. (2016). 'Refusing to Be a Man': Gender, Feminism and Queer Identity in the Punk Culture. *Punk & Post Punk*. 5(3), 247–264.

Austin, A. Craig, S.L. Navega, N. and McInroy, L.B. (2020). It's My Safe Space: The Life-Saving Role of the Internet in the Lives of Transgender and Gender Diverse Youth. *International Journal of Transgender Health*. 21(1), 33–44. DOI: 10.1080/15532739.2019.1700202

Backstrom, A. (2013). Gender Manoeuvring in Swedish Skateboarding: Negotiations of Femininities and the Hierarchical Gender Structure. *Young*. 21(1), 29–53.

Barron, L. (2017). *Tattoo Culture: Theory and Contemporary Contexts*. Rowman & Littlefield.

Baumann, C. Timming, A. and Gollan, P. (2016). Taboo Tattoos? A Study of the Gendered Effects of the Body Art on Consumers' Attitudes Toward Visibly Tattooed Front Line Staff. *Journal of Retailing and Consumer Services*. 29, 31–39.

Becker, H. (1966). *Outsiders: Studies in the Sociology of Deviance*. Free Press.

Berg Olsen, M. (2018, June 18). Tattoo Artist Has Launched His Own #MeToo Movement against the Tattoo Industry. *Metro*. available: https://metro.co.uk/2018/06/18/tattoo-artist-launched-metoo-movement-tattoo-industry-7632945/

Bonell, S. Barlow, F.K. and Griffiths, S. (2021). The Cosmetic Surgery Paradox: Toward a Contemporary Understanding of Cosmetic Surgery Popularisation and Attitudes. *Body Image*. 38, 230–240.

Bordo, S. (1993). *Unbearable Weight: Feminism, Western Culture, and the Body*. University of California Press.

Bordo, S. (1997). The Body and the Reproduction of Femininity. in Conboy, K. Medina, N. and Stanbury, S. (eds) *Writing on the Body: Female Embodiment and Feminist Theory*. Columbia University Press.

Boyle, K. (2019). *#MeToo, Weinstein and Feminism*. Palgrave Macmillan.

Braunberger, C. (2000). Revolting Bodies: The Monster Beauty of Tattooed Women. *Feminist Formations*. 12(2), 1–23.

Bristow, T. (2020, June 4). Tattoo Artists Quit after Claims of Inappropriate Behaviour to Women. *Eastern Daily Press*. available: https://www.edp24.co.uk/news/20754795.tattoo-artists-quit-claims-inappropriate-behaviour-women/

Breeze, M. (2013). Analysing "Seriousness" in Roller Derby: Speaking Critically with the Serious Leisure Perspective. *Sociological Research Online*. 18(4), 23–43.

Breeze, M. (2015). *Seriousness and Women's Roller Derby: Gender, Organization, and Ambivalence*. Palgrave Macmillan.

Broad, K.L. (2001). The Gendered Unapologetic: Queer Resistance in Women's Sport. *Sociology of Sport Journal*. 24(2), 127–144.

Bridges, T. (2009). Gender Capital and Male Body Builders. *Body & Society*. 15(1), 83–107.

Brill, D. (2007). Gender, Status and Subcultural Capital in the Goth Scene. in Hodkinson, P. and Deicke, W. (eds) *Youth Cultures: Scenes, Subcultures and Tribes*. Routledge.

Brown, A. (2007). Rethinking the Subcultural Commodity: The Case of Heavy Metal T-shirt Culture(s). in Hodkinson, P. and Deicke, W. (eds) *Youth Cultures: Scenes, Subcultures and Tribes*. Routledge.

Clarke, J. Hall, S. Jefferson, T. and Roberts, B. (2006). Subcultures, Cultures and Class. in Hall, S. and Jefferson, J. (eds) *Resistance through Rituals: Youth Subcultures in Post-war Britain* (second edition). Routledge.

Cohn, C. (1993). Wars, Wimps and Women: Talking Gender and Thinking War. in Cooke, M. (ed) *Gendering War Talk*. Princeton University Press.

Coles, D. (2016, May 25). Cultural Appropriation and Tattoos. *Spiral Nature.com*. available: www.spiralnature.com/spirituality/cultural-appropriation-tattoos/

Connell, R.W. and Messerschmidt, J. (2005). Hegemonic Masculinity: Rethinking the Concept. *Gender & Society*. 19(6), 829–859.

Craighead, C. (2011). (Monstrous) Beauty (Myths): The Commodification of Women's Bodies and the Potential for Tattooed Subversions. *Agenda: Empowering Women for Gender Equity*. 25(4), 42–49.

Dann, C. (2018). Constructions of Regulation and Social Norms of Tattooed Female Bodies. in Holland, S. and Spracklen, K. (eds) *Subcultures, Bodies and Spaces*. Emerald Publishing Limited.

Dann, C. (2021). *Navigating Tattooed Women's Bodies Intersections of Class and Gender*. Emerald Publishing Limited.

Dann, C. and Callaghan, J. (2017). Embodiment and Excess: Constructions of Tattooed Mothers in the UK. *Psychology of Women's Review*. 1466–3724.

Davis, K. (1995). *Reshaping the Female Body. The Dilemma of Cosmetic Surgery*. Routledge.

Davis, K. (1997). Cosmetic Surgery as Feminist Utopia? *European Journal of Women's Studies*. 4(1), 23–37.

DeMello, M. (1995). "Not Just for Bikers Anymore": Popular Representations of American Tattooing. *Journal of Popular Culture*. 29, 37–52.

DeMello, M. (2000). *Bodies of Inscription: A Cultural History of the Modern Tattoo Community*. Duke University Press.

De Montfort, P. et al. (2016). Still Invisible? Women Artists in British Public Collections. *britishartstudies.ac.uk*. available: www.britishartstudies.ac.uk/issues/issue-index/issue-2/still-invisible [accessed 10.07.2017].

Deutsch, N.L. (2004). Positionality and the Pen: Reflections on the Process of Becoming a Feminist Researcher and Writer. *Qualitative Inquiry*. 10(6), 885–902. DOI: 10.1177/1077800404265723

Dinçer, P. (2019). Being an Insider and/or Outsider in Feminist Research: Reflexivity as a Bridge between Academia and Activism. *Manas Sosyal Araştırmalar Dergisi*. 8(4), 3728–3745.

DiMaggio, P. (1987). Classification in Art. *American Sociological Review*. 52, 440–455.

Doane, M.A. (1997). Film and the Masquerade: Theorizing the Female Spectator. in Conboy, K. Medina, N. and Stanbury, S. (eds) *Writing on the Body: Female Embodiment and Feminist Theory*. Columbia University Press.

Downes, J. (2012). The Expansion of Punk Rock: Riot Grrrl Challenges to Gender Power Relations in British Indie Music Subcultures. *Women's Studies*. 41(2), 204–237.

Dupont, T. (2014). From Core to Consumer: The Hierarchy of the Skateboard Scene. *Journal of Contemporary Ethnography*. 43(5), 556–581.

Elias, N. (1991). *The Society of Individuals*. Basil Blackwell.

Entwistle, J. and Wissinger, E. (2006). Keeping up Appearances: Aesthetic Labour in the Fashion Modelling Industries of London and New York. *The Sociological Review*. 54(4), 774–794.

Evans, C. and Thornton, M. (1989). *Women and Fashion: A New Look*. Quartet Books.

Farren, M. (2020, December 7). Inside the Toxic Tattoo Industry: From Nazi Symbols to Sexual Assault. *Dazed Magazine*. available: https://www.dazeddigital.com/beauty/article/51184/1/tattoo-metoo-industry-reform-nazi-symbols-racism-sexual-assault-accountability

Ferreira, V. (2011). Becoming a Heavily Tattooed Young Body: From a Bodily Experience to a Body Project. *Youth & Society*. 46(3), 303–337.

Fileborn, B. and Loney-Howes, R. (2019). Introduction: Mapping the Emergence of #MeToo. in Fileborn, B. and Loney-Howes, R. (eds) *#MeToo and the Politics of Social Change*. Palgrave Macmillan.

Finley, N.J. (2010). Skating Femininity: Gender Manoeuvring in Women's Roller Derby. *Journal of Contemporary Ethnography*. 39(4), 359–387.

Fisher, J. (2002). Tattooing the Body, Marking Culture. *Body & Society*. 8(9), 1–107.

Force, W.R. (2022). Tattooing in the Age of Instagram. *Deviant Behavior*. 43(4), 415–431. DOI: 10.1080/01639625.2020.1801176

Fox, K. (1987). Real Punks and Pretenders: The Social Organization of a Counterculture. *Journal of Contemporary Ethnography*. 16(3), 344–370.

Frederick, C.M. and Bradley, K.A. (2000). A Different Kind of Normal? Psychological and Motivational Characteristics of Young Adults Tattooers and Body Piercers. *North American Journal of Psychology*. 2(2), 380–394.

Garrison, E.D. (2000). U.S. Feminism—Grrrl Style! Youth (Sub)cultures and the Technologics of the Third Wave. *Feminist Studies*. 26(1), 141–170.

Gerson, J.M. and Peiss, K. (1985). Boundaries, Negotiation, Consciousness: Reconceptualising Gender Relations. *Social Problems*. 32(4), 317–331.

Gimlin, D. (1996). Pamela's Place: Power and Negotiation in the Hair Salon. *Gender & Society*. 10(5), 505–526.

Gimlin, D. (2006). The Absent Body Project: Cosmetic Surgery as a Response to Bodily Dys-appearance. *Sociology*. 40(4), 699–716.

Gimlin, D. (2010). Imagining the Other in Cosmetic Surgery. *Body & Society*. 16, 57.

Glassner, B. (1995). In the Name of Health. in Bunton et al. (eds) *The Sociology of Health Promotion: Critical Analyses of Consumption, Lifestyle and Risk*. Routledge.

Glucksmann, M. (1994). The Work of Knowledge and the Knowledge of Women's Work. in Maynard, M. and Purvis, J. (eds) *Researching Women's Lives from a Feminist Perspective*. Taylor & Francis.

Grossberg, L. (1992). *We Gotta Get Out of This Place: Popular Conservatism and Postmodern Culture*. Routledge.

Haenfler, R. (2004). Rethinking Subcultural Resistance: Core Values of the Straight Edge Movement. *Journal of Contemporary Ethnography*. 33(4), 406–436.

Halberstam, J. (2003). What's That Smell? Queer Temporalities and Subcultural Lives. *International Journal of Cultural Studies*. 6(3), 313–333.

Hall, S. and Jefferson, T. (eds) (2006). *Resistance through Rituals: Youth Subcultures in Post-war Britain*. Routledge.

Hebdige, D. (1979). *Subculture: The Meaning of Style*. Routledge.

Hochschild, A. (1983). *The Managed Heart*. University of California Press.

Hochschild, A. (2003). *The Commercialization of Intimate Life: Notes from Home and Work*. University of California Press.

Hockin-Boyers, H. Jamie, K. and Pope, S. (2020). Moving beyond the Image: Theorising 'Extreme' Female Bodies. *Women's Studies International Forum*, 83.

Hodkinson, P. (2002). *Goth: Identity, Style and Subculture*. BERG.

Hodkinson, P. (2016). Youth Cultures and the Rest of Life: Subcultures, Post-subcultures and beyond. *Journal of Youth Studies*. 19(5).

Holland, S. (2004). *Alternative Femininities: Body, Age, Identity*. BERG.

Holland, S. (2018). *Modern Vintage Homes & Leisure Lives: Ghosts & Glamour*. Palgrave Macmillan.

Holland, S. and Harpin, J. (2015). Who Is the 'Girly' Girl? Tomboys, Hyper-Femininity and Gender. *Journal of Gender Studies*. 24(3), 293–309.

hooks, b. (1989). *Talking Back: Thinking Feminist, Thinking Black*. South End Press.

Hracs, B. and Leslie, D. (2014). Aesthetic Labour in Creative Industries: The Case of Independent Musicians in Toronto, Canada. *Area*. 46(1), 66–73.

Huppatz, K. (2009). Reworking Bourdieu's "Capital": Feminine and Female Capitals in the Field of Paid Caring Work. *Sociology*. 43(1), 45–66.

Iqbal, N. (2017, March 14). Life at the Sharp End: Jessie Knight, Britain's First Tattoo Artist. *The Guardian*. available: www.theguardian.com/lifeandstyle/2017/mar/14/jessie-knight-britains-first-female-tattoo-artist [accessed 14.03.2017].

Inkluded.com – now unavailable.

Irwin, K. (2003). Saints and Sinners: Elite Tattoo Collectors and Tattooists as Positive and Negative Deviants. *Sociological Spectrum*. 23, 27–57.

James, N. (2016). Using Email Interviews in Qualitative Educational Research: Creating Space to Think and Time to Talk. *International Journal of Qualitative Studies in Education*. 29(2), 150–163. DOI: 10.1080/09518398.2015.1017848

Jensen, S.Q. (2006). Rethinking Subcultural Capital. *Young: Nordic Journal of Youth Research*. 14(3), 257–276.

Jones, J. (2021, November 10). Tattoo's #MeToo. *Rising East*. available: https://risingeast.co.uk/tattoos-metoo/

Kelly, A. (2014, November 16). "I Carried His Name on My Body for Nine Years": The Tattooed Trafficking Survivors Reclaiming Their Past. *The Guardian.com*. available: https://www.theguardian.com/global-development/2014/nov/16/sp-the-tattooed-trafficking-survivors-reclaiming-their-past

Kelly, D.M. Pomerantz, S. and Currie, D. (2005). Skater Girlhood and Emphasized Femininity: "You Can't Land an Ollie Properly in Heels". *Gender and Education*. 17(3), 229–248.

Kelly, D.M. Pomerantz, S. and Currie, D. (2006). "No Boundaries"? Girls' Interactive, Online Learning about Femininities. *Youth & Society*. 38(1), 3–28.

Kiskaddon, D. (2021). Tattooers at Work: An Emotional and Permanent Body Labor. in Leeds Craig, M. (eds) *The Routledge Companion to Beauty Politics*. Routledge.

Kjaran, J.I. and Jóhannesson, I.A. (2016). Masculinity Strategies of Young Queer Men as Queer Capital. *NORMA*. 11(1), 52–65. DOI: 10.1080/18902138.2016.1143274

Kjeldgaard, D. and Bengtsson, A. (2005). Consuming the Fashion Tattoo. *Advances in Consumer Research*. 32, 172–177.

Klein, M. (1997). Duality and Redefinition: Young Feminism and the Alternative Music Community. in Heywood, L. and Drake, J. (eds) *Third Wave Agenda: Being Feminist, Doing Feminism*. University of Minnesota Press.

Klesse, C. (2007). Racialising the Politics of Transgression: Body Modification in Queer Culture. *Social Semiotics*. 17(3), 275–292. DOI: 10.1080/10350330701448561

Kosut, M. (2000). Tattoo Narratives: The Intersection of the Body, Self-identity and Society. *Visual Sociology*. 15(1), 79–100.

Kosut, M. (2006). An Ironic Fad: The Commodification and Consumption of Tattoos. *Journal of Popular Culture*. 39, 1035–1048.

Kosut, M. (2013). The Artification of Tattoo: Transformations within a Cultural Field. *Cultural Sociology*. 8(2), 142–158.

Krenske, L. and McKay, J. (2000). "Hard and Heavy": Gender and Power in a Heavy Metal Music Subculture. *Gender, Place & Culture: A Journal of Feminist Geography*. 7(3), 287–304.

Lane, D. (2021). *The Other End of the Needle: Continuity and Change among Tattoo Workers*. Rutgers University Press.

LeBlanc, L. (1999). *Pretty in Punk: Girls' Gender Resistance in a Boys' Subculture*. Rutgers University Press.

Lees, S. (1993). *Sugar and Spice: Sexuality and Adolescent Girls*. Penguin.

Leong, L. (1992). Cultural Resistance: The Cultural Terrorism of British Male Working-Class Youth. *Current Perspectives in Social Theory*. 12, 29–58.

Letherby, G. (2003). *Feminist Research in Theory and Practice*. Open University Press.

Letherby, G. and Zdrodowski, D. (1995) "Dear Researcher": The Use of Correspondence as a Method within Feminist Qualitative Research. *Gender & Society*. 9(5), 576–593. available: www.jstor.org/stable/189897

Linabary, J.R. Corple, D.J. and Cooky, C. (2020). Feminist Activism in Digital Space: Postfeminist Contradictions in #WhyIStayed. *New Media & Society*. 22(10), 1827–1848.

Lodder, M. (2022). A Medium, Not a Phenomenon: An Argument for an Art-Historical Approach to Western Tattooing. in Martell, J. and Larsen, E. (eds) *Tattooed Bodies. Palgrave Studies in Fashion and the Body*. Palgrave Macmillan. DOI: 10.1007/978-3-030-86566-5_2

Lohman, K. (2022). Creating a Safer Space: Being Safe and Doing Safety in Queer and Feminist Punk Scenes*. *The Sociological Review*. DOI: 10.1177/00380261221092519

Lokke, M. (2013, January 15). A Secret History of Women and Tattoo. *The New Yorker*. available: https://www.newyorker.com/culture/photo-booth/a-secret-history-of-women-and-tattoo

Lovell, T. (2000). Thinking Feminism with and against Bourdieu. *Feminist Theory*. 1, 11–32.

Lundberg, L. (2016). Tattooists Who Have Had Enough of Sexism Open Feminist Studio. available: www.stockholmdirekt.se/

Mahmood, S. (2005). *Politics of Piety: The Islamic Revival and the Feminist Subject*. Princeton University Press.

Marcus, S. (2010). *Girls to the Front*. Harper Perennial.

Maynard, M. (1994). Methods, Practice and Epistemology: The Debate about Feminism and Research. in Maynard, M. and Purvis, J. (eds) *Researching Women's Lives from a Feminist Perspective*. Taylor & Francis.

Marshall, K. Chamberlain, K. and Hodgetts, D. (2019). Female Bodybuilders on Instagram: Negotiating an Empowered Femininity. *Feminism & Psychology*. 29(1), 96–119. DOI: 10.1177/0959353518808319

McCall, L. (1992). Does Gender Fit? Bourdieu, Feminism, and Conceptions of Social Order. *Theory and Society*. 21, 837–867.

McDowell, L. (1997). *Capital Culture: Gender at Work in the City*. Blackwell.

McRobbie, A. and Garber, J. (1991). Girls and Subcultures. in McRobbie, A. (ed) *Feminism and Youth Culture: From Jackie to Just Seventeen*. Routledge.

McRobbie, A. (ed) (1991). *Feminism and Youth Culture: From Jackie to Just Seventeen*. London: Routledge.

McRobbie, A. (1993). Shut up and Dance: Youth Culture and Changing Modes of Femininity. *Cultural Studies*. 7(3), 406–426.

McRobbie, A. and Garber, J. (2006). Girls and Subcultures. in Hall, S. and Jefferson, T. (eds) *Resistance through Rituals: Youth Subcultures in Post-war Britain*. Routledge.

Mears, A. (2011). *Pricing Beauty: The Making of a Fashion Model*. California Press.

Mendes, K. (2015). *SlutWalk: Feminism, Activism and Media*. Palgrave MacMillan.

Mendes, K. and Ringrose, J. (2019). Digital Feminist Activism: #MeToo and the Everyday Experiences of Challenging Rape Culture. in Fielborn, B. and Loney-Howes, R. (eds) *#MeToo and the Politics of Social Change* (pp. 37–51). Palgrave Macmillan.

Messerschmidt, J. (2002). On Gang Girls, Gender and a Structured Action Theory: A Reply to Miller. *Theoretical Criminology*. 6(4), 461–475.

Mifflin, M. (2013). *Bodies of Subversion: A Secret History of Women and Tattoo*. PowerHouse Books.

Mifflin, M. (2014). Ink Sessions. *aeon.co*. available: https://aeon.co/essays/meet-the-tattooist-who-is-both-an-artist-and-a-therapist

Modesti, S. (2008). Home Sweet Home: Tattoo Parlors as Postmodern Spaces of Agency. *Western Journal of Communication*. 72(3), 197–212. DOI: 10.1080/10570310802210106

Monaghan, L. (1999). Creating "The Perfect Body": A Variable Project. *Body & Society*. 5(2–3), 267–290.

Moore, R. (2005). Alternative to What? Subcultural Capital and the Commercialization of a Music Scene. *Deviant Behavior*. 26(3), 229–252.

Moore, R. (2007). Friends Don't Let Friends Listen to Corporate Rock: Punk as a Field of Cultural Production. *Journal of Contemporary Ethnography*. 36(4), 438–474.

Morgan, K.P. (1991). Women and the Knife: Cosmetic Surgery and the Colonization of Women's Bodies. *Hypatia*. 6(3), 25–53.

Morgan, K.P. (1998). Contested Bodies, Contested Knowledges: Women, Health, and the Politics of Medicalization. in Sherwin, S. (ed) *The Politics of Women's Health*. Temple University Press.

Morris, A. (2019). *The Politics of Weight: Feminist Dichotomies of Power in Dieting*. Palgrave Macmillan. DOI: 10.1007/978-3-030-13670-3_6

Muggleton, D. (2000). *Inside Subculture: The Postmodern Meaning of Style*. BERG.

Mullaney, J.L. (2007). "Unity Admirable but Not Necessarily Heeded": Going Rates and Gender Boundaries in the Straight Edge Hardcore Music Scene. *Gender & Society*. 21(3), 384–408.

Mullin, A. (2003). Feminist Art and the Political Imagination. *Hypatia*. 18(4), 189–213.

Munroe, A. (1999). *Women, Work and Trade Unions*. Mansell.

Nordstrom, S. and Herz, M. (2013). "It's a Matter of Eating or Being Eaten": Gender Positioning and Difference Making in the Heavy Metal Subculture. *European Journal of Cultural Studies*. 16(4), 453–467.

O'Neal, E.N. (2019). "Victim Is Not Credible": The Influence of Rape Culture on Police Perceptions of Sexual Assault Complainants. *Justice Quarterly*. 36(1), 127–160. DOI: 10.1080/07418825.2017.1406977

Osterud, A.K. (2009). *The Tattooed Lady: A History*. Speck Press.

Pavlidis, A. (2012). From Riot Grrrls to Roller Derby? Exploring the Relations between Gender, Music and Sport. *Leisure Studies*. 31(2), 165–176.

Pettinger, L. (2010). Brand Culture and Branded Workers: Service Work and Aesthetic Labour in Fashion Retail. *Consumption, Markets and Culture*. 7(2), 165–184.

Pettinger, L. (2005). Gendered Work Meets Gendered Goods: Selling and Service in Clothing Retail. *Gender, Work and Organization*. 12(5), 460–478.

Phipps, A. Ringrose, J. Renold, E. and Jackson, C. (2018). Rape Culture, Lad Culture and Everyday Sexism: Researching, Conceptualizing and Politicizing New Mediations of Gender and Sexual Violence. *Journal of Gender Studies.* 27(1), 1–8. DOI: 10.1080/09589236.2016.1266792

Piano, D. (2003). Resisting Subjects: DIY Feminism and the Politics of Style in Subcultural Production. in Muggleton, D. and Weinzierl, R. (eds) *The Post-subcultures Reader.* BERG.

Pitts, V. (2003). *In the Flesh: The Cultural Politics of Body Modification.* Palgrave Macmillan.

Pitts, V. (1998). "Reclaiming" the Female Body: Embodied Identity Work, Resistance and the Grotesque. *Body & Society.* 4(3), 67–84.

Pitts, V. (1999). Body Modification, Self-Mutilation and Agency in Media Accounts of a Subculture. *Body & Society.* 5(2–3), 291–303.

Pitts, V. (2005). Visibly Queer: Body Technologies and Sexual Politics. *The Sociology Quarterly.* 41(3), 443–463.

Ramazanoglu, C. and Holland, J. (2002). *Feminist Methodology.* SAGE.

Reay, D. (2004). Gendering Bourdieu's Concept of Capitals? Emotional Capital, Women and Social Class. in Adkins, L. and Skeggs, B. (eds) *Feminism after Bourdieu.* Blackwell Publishing.

Reddington, H. (2003). "Lady" Punks in Bands: A Subculturette? in Muggleton, D. and Weinzierl, R. (eds) *The Post-subcultures Reader.* BERG.

Reich, C.M., Anderson, G.D. and Maclin, R. (2022). Why I Didn't Report: Reasons for Not Reporting Sexual Violence as Stated on Twitter. *Journal of Aggression, Maltreatment & Trauma.* 31(4), 478–496.

Renold, E. (2005). *Girls, Boys and Junior Sexualities: Exploring Children's Gender and Sexual Relations in the Primary School.* Routledge.

Richards, A. (2015, July 25). Cultural Appropriation and Tattoos. *th-ink.co.uk.* available: www.th-ink.co.uk/2015/07/25/cultural-appropriation-and-tattoos/

Rivers, N. (2017). *Postfeminism[s] and the Arrival of the Fourth Wave.* Palgrave Macmillan.

Ross-Smith, A. and Huppatz, K. (2010). Management, Women and Gender Capital. *Gender, Work and Organization.* 17(5), 547–566.

Russo, M. (1997). Female Grotesques: Carnival and Theory. in Conboy, K. Medina, N. and Stanbury, S. (eds) *Writing on the Body: Female Embodiment and Feminist Theory.* Columbia University Press.

Sanders, C. (1989). *Customizing the Body: The Art and Culture of Tattooing.* Temple University Press.

Savigny, H. (2021). *Cultural Sexism: The Politics of Feminist Rage in the #MeToo Era.* Bristol University Press.

Scharff, C. (2010). Young Women's Negotiations of Heterosexual Conventions: Theorizing Sexuality in Constructions of the Feminist. *Sociology.* 44(5), 827–843.

Scharff, C. (2016). The Psychic Life of Neoliberalism: Mapping the Contours of Entrepreneurial Subjectivity. *Theory, Culture & Society.* 33(6), 107–122.

Schilt, K. (2004). "Riot Grrrl Is...": The Contestation Over Meaning in a Music Scene. in Bennett, A. and Peterson, R.A. (eds) *Music Scenes: Local, Translocal, and Virtual.* Vanderbilt University Press.

Schippers, M. (2002). *Rockin' Out of the Box: Gender Manoeuvring in Alternative Hard Rock.* Rutgers University Press.

Schippers, M. (2007). Recovering the Feminine Other: Masculinity, Femininity, and Gender Hegemony. *Theory and Society*. 36(1), 85–102.

Scraton, S. Fasting, K. Pfister, G. and Bunuel, A. (1999). It's Still a Man's Game? *International Review for the Sociology of Sport*. 34(2), 99–111.

Shapiro, R. and Heinich, N. (2012). When Is Artification? *Contemporary Aesthetics*. 4. available: www.contempaesthetics.org/newvolume/pages/article.php?articleID=639

Sheane, S. (2012). Putting on a Good Face: An Examination of the Emotional and Aesthetic Roots of Presentational Labour. *Economic and Industrial Democracy*. 33, 145–158.

Shilling, C. (1993). *The Body and Social Theory*. SAGE.

Skeggs, B. (2001). The Toilet Paper: Femininity, Class and Mis-recognition. *Women's Studies International Forum*. 24, 295–307.

Skeggs, B. (1997). *Formations of Class and Gender*. SAGE.

Snape, A. (2020, June 9). This Isn't a Boys' Club Anymore. *Things and Ink*. available: https://www.th-ink.co.uk/category/tattoometoo/

Stahl, G. (2003). Tastefully Renovating Subcultural Theory: Making Space for a New Model. in Muggleton, D. and Weinzierl, R. (eds) *The Post-Subcultures Reader*. BERG.

Swami, V. and Furnham, A. (2007). Unattractive, Promiscuous and Heavy Drinkers: Perceptions of Women with Tattoos. *Body Image*. 4(4), 343–352.

Sweetman, P. (1999). Marked Bodies, Oppositional Identities? Tattooing, Piercing and the Ambiguity of Resistance. in Roseneil, S. and Seymour, J. (eds) *Practicing Identities*. Macmillan.

Thirks, K. (2016). *Love/Hate Zine*. available: http://lovehatezine.bigcartel.com/

Thompson, B.Y. (2015). *Covered in Ink Tattoos, Women, and the Politics of the Body*. NYU Press.

Thompson, B.Y. (2019). LA Ink: Tattooing, Gender, and the Casual Leisure of Tattoo Television. *International Journal of the Sociology of Leisure*. 2, 301–316. DOI: 10.1007/s41978-018-00026-8

Thornton, S. (1995). *Club Cultures: Music, Media and Subcultural Capital*. Polity Press.

Trice, H. (1993). *Occupational Subcultures in the Workplace*. ILR Press.

Tundel, N. (2015, July 2). All-Female Tattoo Shop Makes Its Mark in Male-Dominated Field. available: www.mprnews.org. https://www.mprnews.org/story/2015/07/02/allfemale-tattoo-shop-makes-its-mark-in-maledominated-field

Turley, E. and Fisher, J. (2018). Tweeting Back while Shouting Back: Social Media and Feminist Activism. *Feminism & Psychology*. 28(1), 128–132.

Tseelon, E. (1995). *The Masque of Femininity*. SAGE.

Vail, A. (2000). Slingin' Ink or Scratching Skin? Producing Culture and Claiming Legitimacy among Fine Art Tattooists. *Current Research on Occupations and Professions*. 11:55–73.

Vail, A. (1999). Tattoos are Like Potato Chips…You Can't Have Just One: The Process of Becoming and Being a Collector. *Deviant Behavior*. 20, 253–273.

Veldhuis, C.B. Drabble, L. Riggle, E. Wootton, A.R. and Hughes, T.L. (2018). "I Fear for My Safety, but Want to Show Bravery for Others": Violence and Discrimination Concerns among Transgender and Gender-Nonconforming Individuals after the 2016 Presidential Election. *Violence and Gender*. 26–36. DOI: 10.1089/vio.2017.0032

Velliquette, A.M. Murray, J.B. and Creyer, E.H. (1998). The Tattoo Renaissance: An Ethnographic Account of Symbolic Consumer Behaviour. *Advances in Consumer Research.* 25, 461–467.

Vroomen, L. (2002). *This Woman's Work: Kate Bush, Female Fans and Practices of Distinction.* Unpublished Ph.D. Thesis. University of Warwick.

Warhurst, C. and Nickson, D. (2007). Employee Experience of Aesthetic Labour in Retail and Hospitality. *Work, Employment & Society.* 21(1), 103–120.

Watson, J. (1998). "Why Did You Put *That There?*": Gender, Materialism and Tattoo Consumption. *Advances in Consumer Research.* 25, 453–460.

Weinberg, A. (2017, January 8). Mount Vernon Tattoo Shop Defies Norms of Male-Dominated Field. available: www.spokesman.com. https://www.spokes man.com/stories/2017/jan/08/mount-vernon-tattoo-shop-defies-norms-of-male-domi/

Wicks, D. and Grandy, G. (2007). What Cultures Exist in the Tattooing Collectivity? Ambiguity, Membership and Participation. *Culture and Organization.* 13, 349–363.

Wilkins, A.C. (2004). "So Full of Myself as a Chick": Goth Women, Sexual Independence, and Gender Egalitarianism. *Gender & Society.* 18(3), 328–349.

Williams, D.J. Thomas, J. and Christensen, C. (2014). "You Need to Cover Your Tattoos!": Reconsidering Standards of Professional Appearance in Social Work. *Social Work.* 59(4), 373–375.

Wilz, K. (2019). *Resisting Rape Culture through Pop Culture: Sex after #MeToo.* Lexington Books, ProQuest Ebook Central. available: http://ebookcentral. proquest.com/lib/warw/detail.action?docID=5984664

Witz, A. Warhurst, C. and Nickson, D. (2003). The Labour of Aesthetics and the Aesthetics of Organization. *Organization.* 10(1), 33–54.

Wolf, N. (1990). *The Beauty Myth.* Chatto and Windus.

Wolkowitz, C. (2006). *Bodies at Work.* SAGE.

Woodward, R. (2014, October 12). Female Tattoo Artist Show. available: https:// www.th-ink.co.uk/. https://www.th-ink.co.uk/?s=Female+Tattoo+Artist+Show

Wughalter, E. (1978). Ruffles and Flounces: The Apologetic in Women's Sports. *Frontiers: A Journal of Women's Studies.* 3(1), 11–13.

Index